Teaching
SOCCER

Teaching SOCCER

by

ALAN GIBBON, M.A.

Inspector of Physical Education, Inner
London Education Authority, F.A. Coach

and

JOHN CARTWRIGHT

Manager, England Youth Team
Ex-Coach, Crystal Palace F.C.
F.A. Staff Coach

With a Foreword by

RON GREENWOOD

BELL & HYMAN
LONDON

Published by
BELL & HYMAN LIMITED
Denmark House
37/39 Queen Elizabeth Street
London SE1 2QB

First published in 1972 by G. Bell & Sons Ltd
Reprinted 1973, 1974, 1975
Revised edition 1981

British Library Cataloguing in Publication Data

Gibbon, Alan
  Teaching soccer.
  1. Soccer – Study and teaching
  I. Title   II. Cartwright, John
  796.334′07   GV943

  ISBN 0-7135-1257-1

Printed in Great Britain by
The Camelot Press Ltd, Southampton

Contents

Acknowledgements

We wish to thank the following;

The English Schools' Football Association for permission to reproduce the Advisory Document and Code of Conduct in Appendix 2.

The Headmasters of Lawrence Junior Boys' School, Olga Junior Mixed School, Tower Hamlets, and Lauriston Primary School, Hackney, for their help and co-operation.

Tony Jaffrato, David Brinson and Graham Jones who took the photographs.

Mrs Barbara Fey and Mrs Madge Leaney who did the typing.

Mrs Elizabeth Gibbon for the diagrams and her help and encouragement.

Mrs Naomi Cartwright for her help and encouragement and countless cups of tea.

A. G.

J. C.

Foreword to Second Edition

Like any other subject on the educational curriculum, soccer requires good teaching. Unfortunately, it is often treated differently, for where else would you see advanced theories discussed and applied without the background of fundamental basics? The authors of *Teaching Soccer* make this point regarding basics abundantly clear and, from their experience of the game at ground level, give simple guidelines for the teacher or coach of young players to follow.

We must be sure that the early development of young players is both progressive and realistic and the book will help the teacher to achieve this. The teacher himself should be thoughtful and stimulating and throughout this book these two qualities are encouraged. The young player today is inquisitive, skill hungry, and thirsty for knowledge and information, and the sections on Common Faults and Corrections are invaluable for the teacher and coach. Remember, teaching and coaching are not only concerned with presentation; they also involve spotting faults and correcting them. Then you are really teaching.

Mastery of the basics enables every player to be integrated easily into the more demanding team patterns or planned requirements that the more skilful young player will meet as he progresses in the most popular and wonderful sport in the world. Let us remember that to play well, i.e. with skill and understanding, brings enjoyment to both player and spectator, no matter at what level. This book will encourage and enable both teacher and player to achieve these goals.

RON GREENWOOD

Key to Diagrams

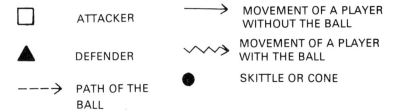

□ ATTACKER

▲ DEFENDER

– – –→ PATH OF THE BALL

⟶ MOVEMENT OF A PLAYER WITHOUT THE BALL

〰〰→ MOVEMENT OF A PLAYER WITH THE BALL

● SKITTLE OR CONE

Preface to Second Edition

When *Teaching Soccer to Boys* was first published it quickly established itself as a standard work for teachers in primary and secondary schools, and the English Schools' Football Association in their 'Advisory Document for Schools' Football for Boys 9–13 Years of Age' especially recommends it to teachers.

We have not felt it necessary to alter the basic structure of the book in this new edition but have updated it in the light of new knowledge we have obtained in working with young players and teachers. It was considered necessary to introduce boys of this age to medium-range passes, though still in small-sided situations, and a clear omission in the old edition was a separate chapter on Shooting. These are the major additions to this new edition, though most chapters have been enlarged or modified.

One last point. The chapter 'For Women Only' in the old edition has been omitted entirely from this edition; many women teachers are now very competent and knowledgeable teachers of soccer and there is no reason why they should not teach the full range of techniques and skills to boys and girls.

A. G.
J. C.

PART ONE: BACKGROUND

1: The Lesson Plan

Most secondary schools allot a double period for the games lesson and the same policy is commonly followed for the older children in junior schools who are reaching the stage when the more general small apparatus lesson of earlier years is giving way to a lesson orientated towards the acquisition of skills for specific games such as soccer.

The lesson is divided into three parts:

A. OPENING ACTIVITY
B. SKILL TRAINING
    i Practice of techniques individually or in small groups without opposition.
    ii Small group practices with opposition.
C. GAMES

A. OPENING ACTIVITY

The boys begin work immediately they enter the playing area whether it be a field, playground or other hard surface area. As many balls as possible, ideally one to each boy, should be available. The boys can either:

(a) practice freely with a ball
or (b) practise a technique suggested by the teacher, probably from work done in the previous lesson.

Practices should be simply organised so that the boys can begin work immediately. Any instructions can be given in the classroom. There should be ample scope for free movement and vigorous activity so that the boys are quickly 'warmed-up'. Although this is essentially an introductory or 'warm-up' stage of the lesson, the practices should be realistic and lead naturally to the next part of the lesson. It is a time when the boys should be encouraged to develop their dribbling skills and mastery of the ball.

Some suitable activities for this part of the lesson are given in Chapter 4.

B. SKILL TRAINING

This is the main teaching part of the lesson. Usually, the teacher will concentrate on a particular aspect of the game, e.g. passing, and introduce a series of progressive practices. The method of progression is explained in more detail in the next chapter but, basically, it is from:

    i small group practices without opposition
to ii small group practices with opposition.

Each aspect of the game is taken in turn and in Part Two of the book suitable practices for each aspect are described in detail.

The teacher's role at this stage of the lesson is absolutely vital, for the boys' skill and understanding of the 'essential nature of the game' will be determined by the teacher's ability to observe faults as they happen and correct them. To help him, we have indicated at every stage common faults that occur and ways of correcting them.

The teacher's intelligent observation is also needed to decide when to progress to another level of difficulty or when to consolidate. One of the crucial and subtle arts of the teacher is to know when to make this decision, either for the whole class or, more probably, for only part of it. We cannot make this decision for him but we have tried to help him to make it.

C. GAMES

The games played should be a natural follow-up from the preceding part of the lesson and can be 'conditioned' in order to focus

OPENING ACTIVITY

SKILL TRAINING

GAMES

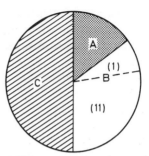

STAGE 3: Improvement continues and
B (1) is reduced further.

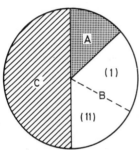

STAGE 1: Introduction of
new technique

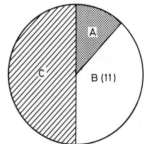

STAGE 4: The whole of the skill
training is devoted to practices
with opposition.

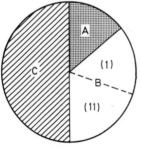

STAGE 2: As the boys improve
less time is devoted to
techniques without opposition.

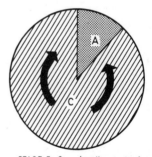

STAGE 5: Occasionally most of
the lesson is devoted to games.

Diagram 1. Development of the lesson.

the attention of the boys, and the teacher, on the aspect of the game that is being tackled. It is during this part of the lesson that the boys attempt to 'transfer' the techniques and skills into actual games of soccer involving small numbers, rarely more than six-a-side. This 'transfer' will be facilitated by the realistic nature of activities in the SKILL TRAINING part of the lesson, which will have involved the boys at all times in decision making and not in teacher-dominated drills.

A number of suitable games for this part of the lesson are described in Chapter 11.

The lesson plan is based upon a double period of about forty minutes' actual playing time, but this will vary from school to school. Whatever the length of the lesson, the plan can be followed.

The plan is flexible and, indeed, it is desirable that the allocation of time within the lesson should vary according to the level of skills of the boys. Thus, when a new aspect of the game is introduced about half of the time in part B of the lesson will be devoted to the practice of techniques without opposition and the other half to practices with opposition. As the skill level rises, more time will be devoted to practices with opposition until the whole of this part of the lesson is taken up with such practices. The balance will be restored when a new skill is introduced.

Diagram 1 shows the development of the lesson during the teaching of a skill.

It is tempting to give some idea of the time the class will spend at each stage or how long they should spend at a skill before they progress to another, but this cannot be done without reference to a particular class. The progress will depend on the ability of the class and the skill and enthusiasm of the teacher. If he follows our suggestions about the *order* of progression in Part Two of this book, and uses his own powers of observation and knowledge of children to decide *when* to progress, we are confident that the boys will grow in skill and gain a knowledge of the 'essential nature of the game'.

2: Presentation of the Work

The way in which a game is taught will be determined by what the teacher hopes to attain with his pupils. The Plowden Report hoped that this would be an awareness of 'the essential nature of the game' and that the method of presenting the work would be planned to promote a genuine understanding of this 'essential nature'.

What then is the 'essential nature' of the game of soccer? Perhaps a definition will help:

Soccer is a passing and running game of an unpredictable and constantly changing pattern, demanding an acute awareness of other players and an ability to make quick decisions and act upon them without delay.

If one adds that the players are usually playing in limited space or 'tight situations' demanding quick and skilful control of the ball, one has probably got deep enough to the heart of the game, to its 'essential nature', to decide what the priorities should be in teaching it to young boys.

The priorities then are the **progressive acquisition of the essential skills (passing, control, heading and challenging), and basic tactics (movement with or without the ball) in realistic situations demanding the making of decisions at every stage.**

In Part Two of the book practices have been carefully devised to help the teacher to concentrate on the priorities. It must be emphasised that these are realistic practices and not 'drills'. They involve:

15

(a) Realism.
(b) The Progressive Acquisition of Skills.

(a) Realism

Whenever possible, a practice should put the boys in situations in which they have to make decisions and solve problems. To achieve this, opposition is necessary. Activities without opposition are of limited value. They do, however, have a place in the programme. Their chief purpose is to 'groove' the movement pattern of a technique before it is placed in a competitive situation. There is some evidence that boys of this age are more willing to practise such 'grooving' than at any other age and if the opportunity is missed it will never return. For this reason, technique practices without opposition are included in Part Two of the book but they are linked at all times to more realistic practices with opposition and take up a progressively smaller amount of time in the programme. They are always carried out with a sense of urgency otherwise any element of realism is lost.

(b) Progressive Acquisition of Skill

The practices in Part Two and the order in which the topics are introduced are intended to form a progressive programme of work. However, the progressive acquisition of skill does not follow a smooth upward curve; it would be convenient if it did. It is affected by a number of factors which the teacher should be aware of if his teaching is to be meaningful.

(i) *Whole and Part Learning*

Some skills, usually very simple ones, can be acquired by practising them whole. Others are far too complicated and are probably best broken down into more understandable parts. The whole game of soccer must obviously be broken down into parts; fortunately the parts it is divided into can themselves be interesting and are easily put back into the whole game.

The whole game of soccer for young schoolboys need not,

indeed should not, be the adult form of soccer with eleven players on each side. This is far too sophisticated a concept for all but the most mature ten-, eleven- or twelve-year-old. Most boys will comprehend better a game involving smaller numbers played on a smaller pitch.

The chief purpose of the practices and small-side games described in Part Two is to allow the boys to enjoy taking part in stimulating and realistic 'parts' in which they are successful and which can be related at all times to a 'whole' they can also understand.

(ii) *Transfer of Training*

The progressive acquisition of game skills would seem to be dependent on the transfer of training from one situation to another, though how this happens and to what extent is still a matter for stringent investigation.

If the situations are similar and the learner perceives the similarity, the transfer is more likely to take place. What is more, if the situations are realistic and involve an appreciation of the true nature and underlying principles of the game, transfer is even more likely to take place.

The practices in Part Two have been devised to facilitate transfer; they demand intelligent involvement and the variation from one practice to another is not very great. They have been modified and refined in the light of experience over a number of years with normal classes of schoolboys from eight different schools.

(iii) *Motivation*

Most boys enjoy playing soccer so that there are few problems in motivating them. However, if there is to be progressive acquisition of skill, the boys must enjoy and see the purpose of practising the parts of the whole game. Soccer, as we have already observed, can be broken down into meaningful and enjoyable parts so that the problem of motivating the boys hardly arises.

Competition is also a powerful motivating force. It must, however, be used intelligently so that every child, regardless of his ability, achieves success. The aim should be to harness the competitive nature of boys to the acquisition of the skills of the game. If a boy can't always be on the winning side he *must not* always be on the losing side. The practices in Part Two *guarantee* that he will have his share of success!

(iv) *Age*

It is not uncommon to see young schoolboys trying to cope with the eleven-a-side game on a full-size pitch. They have not reached a stage of development to cope with such a situation and it says much for this wonderful game that so many boys continue to enjoy it *despite* their experience of it at school.

At about nine or ten years of age it would seem that most boys really become enthusiastic about team games and are prepared to practise hard to acquire success in them. This 'golden age of skill learning' lasts a few years but at about thirteen years of age most boys will have a good idea whether soccer is the activity at which they are going to excel; it may be that some other game or more individual pursuit is more suited to their temperament and ability. They should, however, have the opportunity to realise their own potential during that period of their life when the acquisition of physical skills is easier to achieve and when physical prowess is so important to their social and self-esteem.

Demonstrations

This is an appropriate time to say a little about the use and value of demonstrations. The teacher may find it useful to arrange a demonstration of a particular technique or practice he is introducing to his class. The demonstration can be performed by a skilful group of boys who have practised it briefly before it is shown to the class.

A demonstration may also be used when most of the class is making a particular mistake. The boy or boys who aren't making the mistake can show the others how the technique or practice should be performed.

Demonstrations, however, should be brief and illustrate clearly one, or at the most two, points. They should not interfere with the flow of the lesson. They should, above all, be good demonstrations and be followed immediately by practice.

If the teacher is skilful he can demonstrate techniques himself, but if he is not he will be well advised to find a skilful boy who is capable of giving a satisfactory demonstration. Films, particularly the cassette or loop type, are useful in this context, but unfortunately, they can rarely be followed by immediate practice.

☆   ☆   ☆

The material in Part Two has been planned to provide a progressive scheme of work for the nine to thirteen age group—the 'golden age of skill learning'. During this time the boys will normally be taught in classes of approximately thirty pupils covering the widest range of physical ability. The teachers will often be non-specialists and the material in this book has been prepared to help them.

The coaching situation involving smaller groups of similar ability, the school team perhaps, is beyond the scope of this book, though this is not intended to imply that there is a clear distinction between teaching and coaching. The good coach should always be concerned with basic principles; he should also be concerned with deeper insights that have little relevance to the class teaching situation.

ORDER OF WORK

The heart of the lesson is the SKILL TRAINING. This is divided into:

    i Practice of techniques without opposition.
    ii Small group practices with opposition.

In Part Two of the book practices of both types are described, topic by topic, and are arranged in a progressive way so that the teacher can work systematically through the programme.

The order in which the topics are arranged is not haphazard; they are progressive and each topic contains elements of skill and tactical awareness that are vital to success in the succeeding topic. The correct order of progression from topic to topic is, therefore, intrinsic to success in the programme; for example, success at the second topic, control, will depend on a reasonable level of ability at the first topic, passing.

The starting point for a teacher with a new class can quickly be determined if he assesses their level of skill in five- or six-a-side games. It may, however, be more convenient for the teacher to start from scratch with his new class, whatever their age or level of ability, and then progress quite quickly to a realistic level.

The rate of progression through the programme will depend on the ability of the boys in the small group practices with opposition and not on their ability to perfect isolated technique without opposition.

First Topic: Passing

Passing is the foundation on which the whole structure of soccer is built. The first task for the teacher is to build a firm foundation by raising the standard of passing of his class; everything else that follows will involve this fundamental skill.

The teacher should concentrate on the short pass in the early stages: passes with the inside of the foot, the outside of the foot and the toe-end. As the boys become proficient at short passing they can move on to medium passes, using the inside and outside of the foot. These are the passes most commonly used even in adult games and as the boys will be almost exclusively involved in small-sided games, these passes will predominate. Through the 'short' and 'medium' game the boys will learn the value of accurate passing and ball retention and will not be tempted to use the 'big boot' to get themselves out of trouble. The boys will progress carefully from competitive group situations which are over-loaded to guarantee success, e.g. 7 $v.$ 1, to situations which demand a higher level of skill, e.g. 4 $v.$ 1, 3 $v.$ 1, and 2 $v.$ 1.

The boys should be encouraged to use either foot during the passing practices.

Second Topic: Control

The ability to control the ball quickly and effectively is extremely important and is the next topic to be tackled. It is begun when the teacher is satisfied that most of the boys in the class have reached a reasonable standard of passing in the 4 v. 1 situation. Control is introduced at this stage because it is necessary for success in the smaller groups in which the boys will soon be working, i.e. 3 v. 1 and 2 v. 1.

The types of control most likely to be needed are:

  i Use of the inside of the foot to take the pace off the ball rolling along the ground.

 ii Use of the inside of the foot to take the pace off the low bouncing ball.

iii Use of the abdomen or lower part of the chest to take the pace off the higher bouncing ball.

iv Use of the thigh to take the pace off a dropping ball.

 v Use of the chest to take the pace off a dropping ball.

Third Topic: Basic Tactics

When the small group work in Passing and Control has reached a satisfactory level, it is time to introduce some basic tactical ideas into the programme. All of the teaching *must* be done through small-group practices with opposition, though the occasional use of a blackboard might help to establish tactical ideas.

Until this stage the overloading against the one opponent will have been so great that boys will have been able to achieve reasonable success without moving far when they haven't got the ball. Now in the 3 v. 1 situations, they must learn the importance of:

(a) *Movement without the ball.* Intelligent movement by the boys not in possession is vital if the boy with the ball is to find either of his colleagues with any of the simple passes he has already learned. They must space themselves so that the boy with the ball has passing alternatives and must move into supporting positions around him.

(b) *Calling instructions.* Teachers have often discouraged any talking or shouting in the game of soccer. They have probably been forced into this drastic action because of unnecessary and unhelpful shouting by the boys. This probably reflects the way in which the boys have been taught soccer. In fact, the boys should be encouraged to talk to help each other and call instructions both during the small-group practices and the actual games. If they have learned the game properly they will not call for the ball when they are in bad positions and they will warn a colleague about an impending challenge. A perceptive teacher can soon impress upon the boys the value of intelligent calling.

(c) *Movement with the ball.* The boy in possession must learn to 'attack the space alongside an opponent in order to put him off balance. A wily opponent in the 3 *v*. 1 situation, for example, will soon learn to keep away from the boy with the ball and entice him to make a pass he can intercept. If either of the other two boys does not position himself intelligently the opponent's job will be so much easier. In such a situation the boy with the ball must 'attack' the opponent and commit him to a tackle; he can then pass the ball before the challenge is made or, of course, dribble past the opponent.

Fourth Topic: Heading

Heading is not an easy technique for young boys to acquire and it has been deliberately held back until this stage of the programme when the boys are proficient in some of the techniques more easily acquired by young schoolboys.

It is important that dry, light, well-inflated balls are used for heading practices. The reluctance of many boys, and men, to head a ball can very often be traced back to painful early attempts to head a heavy ball. Fortunately, modern technology has at last rendered the soggy leather ball a thing of the past.

Fifth Topic: Challenging, Dribbling and Movement with and without the Ball

This topic is dealt with at this late stage because:

(a) Most boys are capable, even in the early stages, of making a reasonable effort to gain possession of the ball.

(b) Until this stage it has been necessary to overload the practices against the opponent or challenger so that success is experienced in the positive, creative skills of passing, control, basic tactics and heading. Now the groups can be loaded to give the opponent, or challenger, a chance of success in more realistic situations, i.e. 2 *v*. 1. However, the attackers will have to develop further the techniques of dribbling and running with and without the ball in order to deceive challengers in the 2 *v*. 1 situation.

Sixth Topic: Shooting

The object of soccer is to score goals and the boys will have had numerous opportunities to beat the goalkeeper in the small-game situations they are put into for at least half of every lesson. Although the object of the game is undoubtedly to score goals it is essentially the end product of skilful play and this should be the first aim of the teacher of young schoolboys. Boys should become aware that their team will have many more goal-scoring opportunities if they are prepared to harness their own individual skills to the common purpose of the team, which is to get a player into a goal-scoring position.

The work in Chapter 10 is devoted to the techniques of shooting, which *all* players will need when they find themselves with a scoring opportunity.

FURTHER PROGRESS

By this stage in the programme the boys should have reached quite a high level of skill and further progress will be made by increasing the difficulty of the practices with opposition. Practices without opposition should only be included if the teacher feels that a particular technique is being performed badly in a competitive situation and might be improved by a short period of isolated practice.

The introduction of a second and then a third opponent will create further problems for the boys; not only is there an opponent threatening an immediate challenge but there is a covering opponent not far away. However, the boys will have worked up to this stage realistically and progressively and should possess the skills to cope with this new situation.

The ultimate object of the programme is skilful play in numerically balanced small groups. They will, of course, have been involved in such small-side games from the first but now their involvement will be heightened by skill and understanding.

GOALKEEPING

No attempt is made in this book to stress the roles of particular positions. Young schoolboys should not be encouraged to become position conscious; this is something they will acquire at a later stage.

The position of goalkeeper is, however, unique. It involves quite different techniques from the outfield players and cannot easily be incorporated into a teaching plan. Some boys, from an early age, show a particular aptitude for goalkeeping; others show a passing interest before returning to outfield play.

The work in Chapter Twelve has been arranged so that the techniques of goalkeeping can be integrated into the main body of the work. Practices for goalkeepers are related to each topic, and to each practice where possible, so that opportunities are given at every stage for those boys who think of themselves, temporarily perhaps, as goalkeepers.

3: Facilities and Equipment

The Playing Area

A football field is not necessarily the best place to teach soccer to young schoolboys. During good weather, particularly in the early autumn and late spring, a field is ideal, but for most of the winter a hard surface that drains quickly is needed. It is common for young schoolboys to walk, or be transported by special buses, to muddy, over-used grass pitches where their chance of acquiring or exercising any kind of skill is very remote. They have probably left behind at school a playground that is well suited to the acquisition of soccer skills and they have wasted valuable time in fruitless travelling. It is no accident that even the men who play soccer for a living now do much of their training on hard surfaces; new schools, both secondary and junior, are being planned and built with adjoining all-weather surfaces, very often in addition to the playground. It is not inconceivable that professional soccer will eventually be played on artificial surfaces. Why should mud be an intrinsic part of this skilful and sophisticated game?

Many playgrounds, particularly in the old schools which date back to the turn of the century, have playgrounds ideal for the teaching of soccer and other games. They are often enclosed by high walls which can be used for all kinds of games practices; it is even possible to demonstrate quite clearly what is meant by the 'wall pass'.

It is a pity that the playgrounds of so many modern schools either have no boundary walls whatsoever or are surrounded by wire netting. Worse still, they are sometimes bordered by gardens on which pupils tread at their peril. A high wall along at least one

25

side of a playground is invaluable for games practices; sited properly it can even enhance the aesthetic appearance of the school, for any gardener knows the value of a well-sited wall. Perhaps the poet Robert Frost was referring to educational architects when he wrote 'Something there is that doesn't love a wall'. A keen teacher of games certainly does!

Markings

If the playground is to be used extensively for games it must be marked out properly. The markings will be permanent, so they should be planned with the whole games programme of the school in mind. This will embrace small apparatus lessons for young juniors, rounders, skittleball, padder tennis, cricket, netball, circle games of all kinds, and even games the children invent for themselves. To cater for all these activities the markings should be adaptable and the use of two colours will almost certainly be necessary. A scaled-down version of a full-sized soccer pitch, with goal and penalty areas, is certainly not necessary.

A rectangle divided into eight 10 yard squares can be used for four games of small-side games of soccer (Diagram 2) or for skill training in eight groups (Diagram 3).

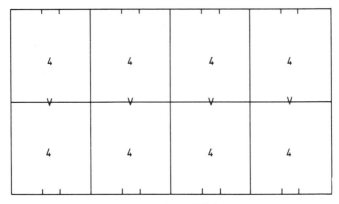

Diagram 2. Class of 32 boys.

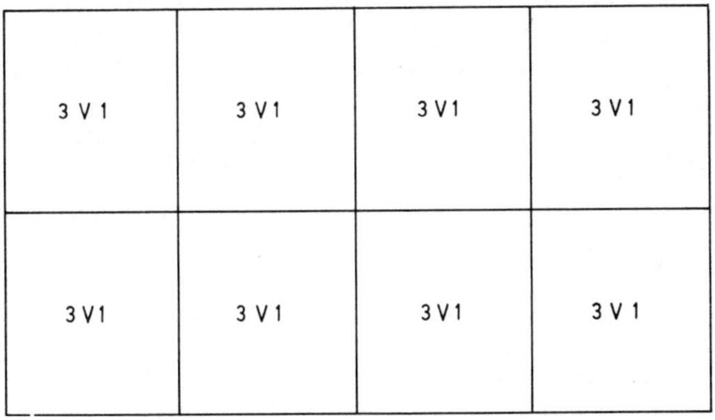

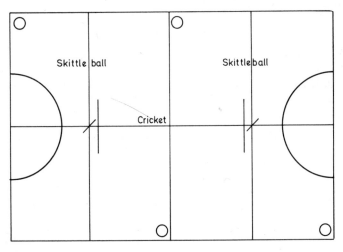

3 V 1
3 V 1
3 V 1
3 V 1
3 V1
3 V 1
3 V 1
3 V 1

Diagram 3

Skittle ball
Skittle ball
Cricket

Diagram 4

The same area can be overmarked with lines of another colour, or with broken lines, to cater for other games (Diagram 4).

Too many markings can cause confusion but this can be avoided if full use is made of even the most apparently inconvenient

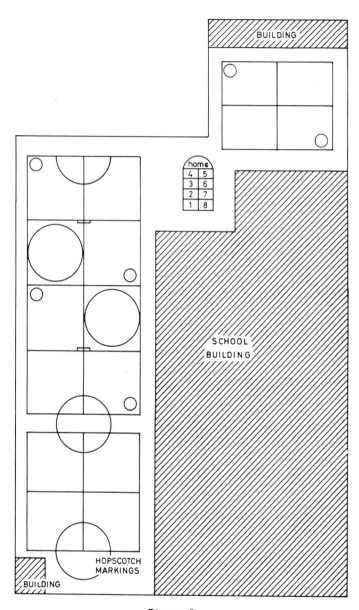

BUILDING

home
4	5
3	6
2	7
1	8

SCHOOL
BUILDING

HOPSCOTCH
MARKINGS

BUILDING

Diagram 5.

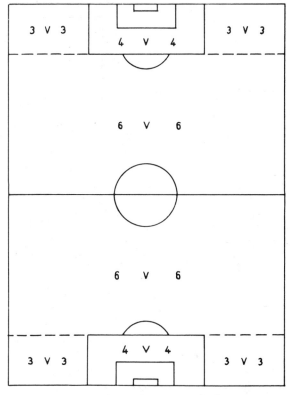

Diagram 6. 64 boys are involved.

corners of the playground and if playground chalk is used to supplement permanent markings.

Diagram 5 shows markings for an awkward-sized playground used by boys and girls. It can be used for skittleball, cricket, net-ball, padder tennis, badminton, circle games and, of course, soccer.

It is important that adequate margins (1 metre) should be left between boundary lines and such hazards as walls, chain link fences, steps, rails, etc.

If a full-sized pitch is used for soccer, much better use can be made of it than by playing an eleven-a-side game. At the very least two games with small numbers can be played across the two halves of the pitch; better still, all the permanent markings can be used

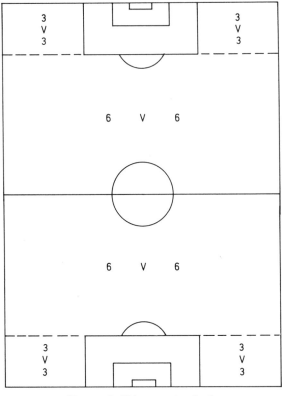

Diagram 7. 48 boys are involved.

for many small-side games (Diagram 6). More often than not the penalty area, and particularly the goal area, is in a very muddy condition and should be avoided (Diagram 7).

If a school is fortunate enough to have a junior-sized pitch (20–25 metres long by 12–15 metres wide) it is ideal for five- or six-a-side football when played in two halves.

Equipment

Balls Ideally, there should be one ball to each boy or at least one between two boys. Even a small junior school, with little money to spend, can build up a good supply of the inexpensive moulded balls that are now available; there are quite a few on the market and all are quite cheap. If they are used on a hard surface they should be slightly under-inflated so that young schoolboys can control them more easily. The colour of the ball is not important, but one advantage of the white ball is that it can be clearly marked with the name of the school, which might prevent it going astray!

Skittles Eight wooden skittles (four colours) will be useful.

Rounders posts The posts with heavy metal bases are very useful as goal posts. Ash staves also make good posts.

Portable posts of tubular steel or wood are useful.

Playground chalk This is very useful to supplement the permanent markings.

Coloured bibs These can be used for the small-group activities and small-side games. Thirty-six of four different colours will be more than enough. They can be made by the girls in the school or perhaps a co-operative group of parents will help. The bibs should be made or bought to fit the boys as those normally available are far too large.

Whistles Boys can be trained to referee the small-side games and a number of whistles should be available for this purpose.

Children's Personal Equipment

It is not too difficult to persuade boys to acquire suitable equipment of their own, as they usually wish to emulate the stars of the professional game and particularly of their own local side. This is one of the better examples of the professional game they can well follow, as the turn-out of professional players is usually immaculate; it is a pity that boys are sometimes allowed to acquire the less desirable habits, appealing to the referee, excessive displays of rejoicing, time wasting, etc.

The most important item is footwear and if the playground or other hard area is used, plimsolls are perfectly suitable and cheap. There are many other, more expensive, soft training shoes on the market which many boys now use.

The boys will not require much persuasion to obtain the shirt, shorts and stockings of their favourite side; such items are popular birthday and Christmas presents from parents and relations.

If there is more than one side which commands the boys' loyalties, the soccer lesson can add a bit of colour to an otherwise drab winter day.

Track suits are becoming more common and are also popular presents from parents and relations. If a boy doesn't have one he should be encouraged to bring an old sweater for use on very cold days.

If a school has showering facilities the boys will normally bring a towel. Most junior schools do not have such facilities but the boys should, if possible, be allowed to wash themselves thoroughly and should bring a towel to school for this purpose. If the washing facilities are inadequate, the flexible arrangements of the normal junior school curriculum might allow them to be used in smaller groups.

PART TWO: CONTENT

Introduction

This part of the book is devoted entirely to descriptions of practices and games. The way in which they are used throughout the programme is explained in Chapters 1 and 2.

Common faults the teacher should look for have been listed after each practice. These are included to assist him in his teaching. Sometimes only one or two boys will make a particular mistake and they can be helped without the flow of the lesson being stopped. At other times most of the children in the class will be faulty in a particular technique. That may be the time to stop the whole class to point out the mistake and possibly watch a demonstration by boys who do not display the fault.

It is important that the practices without opposition are carried out as near match speed as possible, in order to give a sense of realism and to facilitate the transfer of skill to the practices involving opposition. The transfer of skill from the latter practices to the game situation will be facilitated if both are present in each lesson.

4: Opening Activities

It is in this part of the lesson that the boys are encouraged to develop mastery of the ball, particularly the techniques of dribbling and running with the ball. Dribbling is basically the technique of quickly changing direction with the ball to deceive an opponent, whereas the technique of running with the ball involves moving quickly into space with the ball over varying distances.

Practice 1. (Ball to each boy).
The boys dribble the ball anywhere in the playing area.

Common Faults—Corrections
i The ball is kicked too far ahead.

Encourage a 'feel' for the ball by asking the boys to keep it within one yard. 'Imagine the ball is tied to your feet with elastic that won't stretch more than one yard.' (Photo 1)

ii The boys will tend to move the ball from the inside of one foot to the inside of the other; this can lead to restricted movement, particularly when the speed is increased.

Encourage the boys to use the outside as well as the inside of the foot. (Photo 2)

Practice 2. As for the previous practice but the boys are now asked to look around them while still keeping the ball under control (Photo 3). This is a vital skill of soccer and boys should acquire it very early. Soccer is a team game and players must be aware of the movements of players around them. Very young boys

1 (above). Imagine the ball is tied to your feet with elastic that won't stretch more than one yard.

2 (above right). Using the outside of the foot.

3. Looking around with the ball still under control.

will need as much space as possible for this practice but the area can be reduced as skill increases.

Common Faults—Corrections

i The boys keep their eyes on the ball and only look up occasionally.

In fact, they should do the opposite; look around most of the time and at the ball occasionally.

Practice 3. As for the previous practice but the boys are encouraged to change direction. At first they can change direction on a signal from the teacher but later the change can occur naturally as players try to avoid each other. This will be even more necessary when the playing area is reduced. There are many ways of changing direction with a ball and the boys should be encouraged to try some of them:

(a) A foot is put on top of the ball which is dragged back with the sole (Photos 4 and 5).
(b) The boy reaches past the ball with his leg and foot and drags the ball back with the inside of the foot (Photos 6 and 7).
(c) As for (b) but the outside of the foot is used (Photo 8).
(d) The heel is put directly behind the ball. This is a quick, but not easily controlled, way of changing direction (Photo 9).

Common Faults—Corrections

i At first the boys will change direction regardless of other players.

They should be encouraged to change direction only when it is made necessary by the proximity of other boys. The change of direction may be sideways, backwards or diagonally.

ii The boys will tend to change direction from a rather upright stance.

As the change of direction is about to be made the whole body should be lowered by bending the knees.

4 and 5. The ball is dragged back with the sole of the foot.

6 and 7. The ball is dragged back with the inside of the foot.

8. The ball is dragged back with the outside of the foot (page 36).   9. The heel is used to change direction (page 36).

Practice 4. (A ball between two boys, 6–8 metres apart)
The boys pass the ball to each other whilst running anywhere in the playing area. This practice demands accuracy of passing and the boys are forced to make decisions about when to pass and when to hold on to the ball; the development of this skill is dealt with in the chapter on passing.

Practice 5. (A ball between two boys, 6–8 metres apart)
One player, using his right hand, bounces the ball towards the space two to three metres to the left of his partner, now acting as an opponent. As his partner moves sideways to his left to cover the approaching run, he will be off-balance and the player with the ball, when quite close, turns to put his body between his opponent and the ball. He keeps on turning, still using his right hand and moves through the space left by his opponent.

10. The body is put between the opponent and the ball, which is controlled with the outside of the foot furthest from the opponent.

11 and 12. The opponent doesn't move quickly to cover the run, and the player with the ball accelerates past him, still controlling the ball with the foot furthest from the opponent.

If he attacks the space to the right of his opponent he will use his left hand to keep the ball as far away as possible. In this case the opponent will move to his right to cover the space being attacked and the player with the ball, again when quite close, will turn to keep his body between his opponent and the ball and move quickly through the space left by his opponent.

As the boys become proficient using their hands, they attempt the same practice using their feet. The turn to put the body between the opponent and the ball is achieved by using the outside of the foot furthest away from the opponent (Photo 10). If the opponent doesn't move quickly sideways to cover the angled run, the player with the ball can, of course, increase his speed and continue his run past his opponent, still keeping the ball under control with the foot furthest away from his opponent (Photos 11 and 12). On the other hand, if the opponent moves across too far to cover the run, the attacking player, when still a few metres away, can turn into the space left by his opponent.

Common Faults—Corrections

i   The boy with the ball doesn't 'attack' the space 2 or 3 metres to the side of his opponent, so that he isn't thrown moment-arily off-balance by his movement sideways to cover the run.

The attacking boys should be encouraged to make positive runs, but still keeping the ball under control.

ii The boy with the ball turns his body when he is too far away from his opponent.

He should be taught to delay the body turn until he is almost in contact with his opponent. He then 'rolls' off him and through the space he has left. This requires plenty of confidence and lots of practice.

iii The boy with the ball doesn't recognise that his opponent hasn't moved quickly sideways to cover his positive run and continues with his body turn.

13. The defender commits himself too early and the player with the ball drags it across into the open space.

In this case he should increase his speed and continue his run past his opponent.

iv The attacking player doesn't recognise that the defending player has committed himself too early to cover his positive run and again he continues with his turn.

He should now drag the ball across into the space left by his opponent and accelerate through it (Photo 13).

v The attacking player, finding his run blocked, drags the ball across the front of his opponent with the inside of his foot and is easily dispossessed.

He should turn the ball away from his opponent with the outside of his foot.

Practice 6. (A ball each except for 4 or 5 boys)
The boys in possession move anywhere in the playing area and are challenged by the 4 or 5 boys. As well as giving the 4 or 5 boys without a ball plenty of practice in challenging, this practice

ensures that the boys in possession must look around them if they are to avoid being robbed of the ball. They can also practise 'shielding' the ball from the challenger; this simply means keeping the body between the challenger and the ball, a very important aspect of control.

This opening phase of the lesson is a good time to encourage the boys to acquire simple ways of beating an opponent. They can be practised without opposition at first and can later be attempted against opposition. Examples are:

(a) *Change of Speed*

This is the easiest way of beating an opponent. If the opponent does not move sideways quickly enough to cover the diagonal run of the player with the ball, he should increase his pace to accelerate past him.

(b) *Feint Kick and Change of Direction*

The boy with the ball pretends to kick the ball with one foot and moves the ball in the other direction with the inside of the opposite foot.

(c) The boy puts his foot across the ball in one direction and sweeps it away in the opposite direction with the outside of the same foot. In neither (b) nor (c) should the boys expect to deceive the opponent completely; they should aim to put him off balance and then accelerate past him before he recovers. Boys should learn at an early stage that it isn't necessary to 'bamboozle' the opponent completely to get past him. Positive movement towards the space on either side of an opponent will throw him momentarily off-balance: it is then that the dribbling techniques are used to get past him.

There are many other ways of beating an opponent and some boys will acquire them by watching first-class players. The teachers might look out for them and bring them to the attention of the whole class.

At first boys will need as much space as possible to carry out these practices successfully, but as they become more skilful the area in which the boys work can be decreased.

5: Passing

THE PASS WITH THE INSIDE OF THE FOOT

(a) Practice of Techniques without Opposition

Practice 1. (Ball between two boys about 5 metres apart)

The boys pass the ball to each other with the inside of the foot; they should stop it before returning it (Photos 14–16).

Common Faults—Corrections

i   The non-kicking foot is placed too far back.

It should be placed alongside the ball so that the head is over the ball when the pass is made.

ii The non-kicking foot is placed at an angle to the intended line of the pass resulting in an inaccurate pass.

The foot should point in the direction of the pass.

iii The kicking foot is not turned at right angles to the line of the pass, resulting in an inaccurate pass.

iv The ball is not struck centrally with the broadest part of the inside of the foot resulting in a swerving or spinning pass that is difficult to control.

v The follow-through is not in the direction of the pass.

This also causes the ball to spin and the boy finishes in an awkward cross-legged stance that makes a subsequent movement difficult.

vi There is no follow-through; the boy makes a stab at the ball, causing it either (a) to lift off the ground or (b) to shoot away quickly making judgement of the strength of the pass difficult.

14 (above left). Non-kicking foot alongside the ball and pointing in the direction of the pass.

15 (above right). Kicking foot turned at right angles to the line of the pass and ball struck centrally with the broadest part of the foot.

16. Follow through in the direction of the pass.

vii The arms are not used properly to aid balance.

The boys should be encouraged to extend their arms side-ways when making the pass. In the early stages they might exaggerate this movement by holding their arms at shoulder level; they will soon find the level suitable for them.

viii The better foot is used however the ball approaches them.

They should be encouraged to use the left foot to stop and pass the ball approaching the left side and the right foot on the right side.

It is important, particularly in the early stages, that passes are not hit so firmly that the receiver has problems controlling the ball.

Final Teaching Point

The boys should keep their eyes on the ball as they hit it.

Practice 2.   As for Practice 1 except that the boys do not stop the ball before returning it; they make a first-time pass.

Common Faults—Corrections

It is much more difficult to return a moving ball so that the faults already noted in Practice 1 will be magnified and should be corrected.

In addition:

i Many boys will stand still and stretch out their kicking foot towards an inaccurate pass resulting in an even more in-accurate return. They should move quickly so that they get behind an inaccurate pass to line it up for the return.

ii The ball will be returned too strongly. The boys should be encouraged to push rather than hit the ball back. The strength of the pass is determined by the distance it has to travel. It will be difficult for boys to control an over-strength pass.

Practice 3. (Ball between two boys about 5 metres apart)
The boys move anywhere in the playing area and pass the ball to each other with the inside of either foot.

Common Faults—Corrections

i The boys will make first-time return passes even though there is another player in the way.

They should retain the ball in such situations and return it when the way is clear. If there is no other player between them and their opponent they can make a first-time pass.

ii The boys will tend to watch the ball all the way from their partners to their own foot. They will not, therefore, be able to see where their partners have moved to.

They should be taught to look around before receiving the ball (Chapter 4, Practice 2), and even when it is on the way to them. When it does arrive they will already have a good idea whether and where they are going to return it or whether they are going to control it.

iii Many passes will be directed straight at players as they are moving.

Boys should direct passes in front of their partners so that they take them in their stride (Photos 17 and 18). The pass should not, however, be too far in front of a player so that he is forced to sprint after it. At first the boys will use the whole of the playing area but as they become more skilful the area will be reduced so that they are working in more confined situations.

(b) Small Group Practices with Opposition

The teacher must first decide what the size of the groups is to be. If the boys are very young, lacking in skill or new to the teacher, he will be well advised to decide on 7 *v*. 1 groups and progress from there.

The stages of progression are:

17 and 18. The ball is directed into the path of the receiver

STAGE 1

The class is divided into groups of eight boys. One boy from each group is nominated as the opponent to produce 7 *v*. 1 groups. Such over-loading will ensure success for even the most unskilful boys. Each boy takes his turn as the opponent and his job is simply to attempt to intercept the ball as the other seven pass it among themselves. If he gains possession he returns the ball to one of the seven and the practice continues for two minutes when another boy becomes the opponent.

The competitive element can be brought out by either (a) finding which opponent in each group gains the most possession during his two-minute spell or (b) finding which group make the most consecutive passes during a two-minute spell.

Each group is limited to a part of the playing area. This area need not be specifically marked out at this stage, though if the playground has been marked out as suggested in Chapter 3, organisation will be easier.

STAGE 2   Same practice. 6 *v*. 1 groups

STAGE 3   Same practice. 5 *v*. 1 groups; smaller area about 15 metres square.

A class will not always divide conveniently into groups of 8, 7, 6 or 5. For example, a class of 30 might be divided into two groups of 7 *v*. 1 and two groups of 6 *v*. 1. Because of the range of ability in the class it will be sensible in such a situation to put the more skilful boys in the smaller groups. The less skilful boys may take longer to get to the 5 *v*. 1 situation but if the teacher devotes more attention to them than to the more skilful boys, they should not lag far behind. From time to time the teacher can reorganise the groups so that there is at least one very skilful boy in each group; it is amazing what difference he will make. It is important, however, that the usual grouping is according to ability, otherwise skilful boys will either tend to dominate groups or become frustrated with their less skilful fellows.

Common Faults—Corrections

Because of the introduction of an opponent, the boys will find it difficult at first to reproduce the techniques practised without opposition. The teacher must look for the faults already described in the practices without opposition and correct them. Emphasis on correct technique at this stage is vital to further progress.

The presence of an opponent even in this overloaded 7 *v.* 1 situation will cause new problems to arise:

i The ball will be hit immediately, regardless of the position of the opponent.

   The teacher must stress the importance of passing the ball away from the opponent's line of approach. In a 7 *v.* 1 situation the ball can always be directed away from the opponent and it will be unnecessary for the boys to move far; all they need do is space themselves around the opponent.

ii Some boys will be unaware of the distance between themselves and the opponent when they have received or are about to receive the ball; they are therefore unable to decide whether to hold on to the ball or whether to pass it to a colleague quickly.

   The boys must be encouraged to LOOK AROUND THEM; they will then have an idea of the whereabouts of the opponent and can decide whether (a) to hold on to the ball if he is far away (Diagram 8a) or (b) to pass the ball first time if he is fairly near before he can close the passing angle (Diagram 8b). The skill of deciding when to hold and when to pass the ball first-time must be stressed at this stage, because it is a crucial one when the size of the group is reduced.

THE PASS WITH THE OUTSIDE OF THE FOOT

Occasionally, when under pressure from an opponent, a boy will not be able to use the pass with the inside of the foot properly; he will lose vital seconds in trying to make such a pass when a pass with the outside of the foot is more appropriate to the

(A)

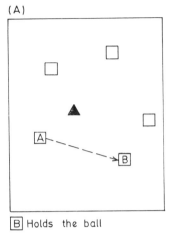

B Holds the ball

(B)

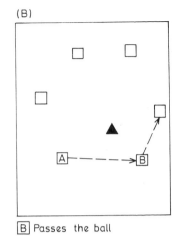

B Passes the ball

Diagram 8a and b

situation (Photos 19 and 20). This new pass is introduced when the boys are reasonably skilful at passing the ball with the inside of the foot in the 5 *v*. 1 situation.

(a) Practice of Techniques without Opposition

Practice 1. (Ball to each boy)
The boys dribble the ball anywhere in the playing area; each time they approach a wall they hit the ball against it with the outside of the foot nearest to the wall.

Practice 2. (Ball between two boys about 6–8 metres apart)
The boys pass the ball to each other with the outside of the foot nearest to the partner, as they run anywhere in the playing area.

In both practices the boys should change direction frequently so that both feet are used.

Common Faults—Corrections
i The non-kicking foot is placed too close to the ball, therefore restricting the kicking movement.

The foot should be placed further to the side than for the

19. Non-kicking foot slightly to the side and ball hit with the side of the foot.

20. Ball taken in the stride and hit to the side with an extended foot. Follow through in the direction of the pass.

pass with the inside of the foot though still almost in line with it. This gives the kicking foot enough room to push the ball away at an angle.

ii The ball is flicked sideways with the side of the foot. Such a pass is difficult to control and cannot be hit with any power. The ball should be taken in the stride and hit towards the side with an extended foot, the contact being made near the base of the small toe. The follow-through then continues along the line of the pass.

(b) Small Group Practices with Opposition

The practices are continued as before, using the 5 v. 1 situation, but now the boys are encouraged to introduce this new pass into their play. It is just as important for the boys to decide which pass to use as to execute it properly. For example, a boy may be controlling the ball with his right foot with the intention of passing it to a colleague on his right with the inside of his left foot; but an opponent makes a quick challenge and the boy, in order to avoid the challenge, decides to pass the ball to his colleague with the outside of his right foot. If, however, the boy is controlling the ball with his left foot when the challenge is made it will be quicker for him to pass the ball to his right with the inside of his left foot.

The teacher should concentrate at this stage on helping the boys to make the correct decisions as well as pointing out and correcting errors of technique.

THE PASS WITH THE TOE-END

It should be understood that the pass with the toe-end is not the full-blooded toe punt, but merely a prod with the toe in order to move the ball away quickly (Photos 21–22). This pass is introduced when the boys are using the pass with the inside and the pass with the outside of the foot reasonably skilfully in the 5 v. 1 situation.

It is an extremely useful pass when a boy is under pressure from an opponent and the ball is not near enough to attempt either of

21. The ball is hit centrally with the toe.
22. The challenger is beaten.

the two previous passes; he merely stretches his leg and prods the ball with his toe in the required direction. It is not an elegant pass but can be very effective.

Common Faults—Corrections

i There is a backswing.

The essence of this pass is speed and there is no time for a backswing.

ii The toe-end contacts the ball to the side resulting in a spinning, understrength and inaccurate pass.

There is little margin of error in this pass and the ball must be hit centrally.

iii The ball is hit too low and the ball lifts off the ground.

iv The ball is hit too high resulting in a 'topped' pass which will be understrength.

Small Group Practices with Opposition

The boys are still working in 5 *v*. 1 groups at this stage and the inclusion of this third type of pass will give them a wider range of passing skills. The SKILL TRAINING part of the lesson at this stage should consist almost entirely of small-group practices with opposition, in which the boys are constantly involved in making decisions as to which pass they must use. The teacher cannot *tell* them; he can only put them into the situation and *help* them.

MEDIUM PASSES

These passes are made over approximately 20 metres by younger boys but can be gradually increased as the boys mature and become more skilful. They can be hit with the inside or outside of the foot and, at this stage, should be kept on the ground. The boys should remember the general rule for most passes:

'Soft and slow is good.'

'Hard and fast is bad.'

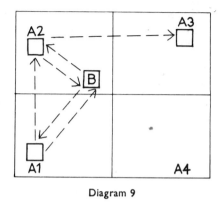

Diagram 9

(a) Practice of Techniques without Opposition

Practice 1 (Ball between five boys in area 20 metres square)
A1 passes the ball to B who returns it.
A1 then either controls it before passing or passes it first time to
A2. A2 repeats the exchange of passes with B before passing to
A3 and so on till all four boys have exchanged passes with B.

The direction of the practice can be reversed so that the boys have
to use both feet. In the early stages the boys may need to control
the ball before passing it, but eventually they will be able to play
most passes first time.

Common Faults—Corrections
  i The boys do not move into the correct position to strike the
     ball with the chosen feet. They should move to the right,
     slightly outside the line of the ball, if the ball is to be passed to
     the left with the right foot (Photo 23).

 ii The ball is struck too firmly, giving the receiving player
     control problems.
     The ball should be struck so that the pace of the ball allows
     the receiving player to pass it comfortably first time.

23. The kicker moves outside the line of the ball to pass the ball on his right. The kicking foot is pulled downwards and the eyes are still on the ball.

24. The kicker moves outside the line of the ball to pass it with the outside of his foot to a colleague on his right.

iii The ball is not struck with the correct part of the foot. The ball should be struck with the foot pulled downwards so that the top of the instep contacts the ball. If the ball is struck too near the toe it will be sliced, and if it is struck too near the ankle it will be hooked.

iv The non-kicking foot is pointing forwards. It should be turned in the direction in which the ball is to be played, otherwise movement will be restricted (Photo 24).

v The ball is struck underneath, causing it to rise too steeply. The ball should be struck about half-way up with the top of the instep.

vi The arms are kept too close to the body. They should be extended to aid balance.

Practice 2. (Ball between five boys in area 20 metres square)
Practice 1 is repeated but using the outside of the foot instead of the instep.

Common Faults—Corrections
All of the faults of the previous practice may occur. In this case the player will have to move slightly further outside the line of the ball to the left in order to direct the ball to the player on the right (Photo 24). The ball is, of course, struck with the top of the outside of the foot.

Practice 3. (Ball between five boys in area 20 metres square)
The previous practice is repeated, except that the ball can be played left or right with the inside or outside of the foot.

Common Faults—Corrections
All of the faults of the previous practices may occur plus the following: the decision about which pass to make is made too late. It must be made early enough for the body to be placed in the correct position to make a technically sound pass.

(b) Small Group Practices with Opposition

The practice is the same as for the practices *without* opposition, except that B, after passing the ball back to A1, now moves in to challenge him. The 4 players try to make four medium passes to each other with B trying to intercept them. If they are successful the practice is repeated.

As the boys become more skilful the A players are asked to achieve more than four consecutive passes. Each player, of course, takes his turn as the challenging player.

Common Faults—Corrections

All the faults of the practices without opposition may occur. In addition:

i The passes are not 'disguised' enough by using the inside and outside of the foot. The challenging player will therefore be able to anticipate obvious passes and put the receiver under pressure.

ii Receiving players make every pass first time.

They should be encouraged to pass first time when under close pressure but control the ball if they find that the challenging players are some distance away.

As the boys improve and the one opponent is being given 'the run around' the practice area for each group can be reduced to about ten metres square and the groups reduced to 4 *v.* 1. Once the boys are coping skilfully with this 4 *v.* 1 situation it is time to move on to the next topic, CONTROL.

6: Control

USING THE INSIDE OF THE FOOT TO TAKE THE PACE OFF THE BALL ROLLING ALONG THE GROUND

(a) Practice of Techniques without Opposition

Practice 1. (Ball between two boys, five to ten metres apart.) The boys pass the ball firmly to each other. They control it with the inside of the foot and return it along the ground (Photos 25–27).

Common Faults—Corrections

i Some boys will stop the ball with the sole of the foot.

This should be discouraged because it is very difficult to judge and the ball is likely to pass under the foot. Even if the boy does judge it correctly he finishes in a static position and the ball is 'dead', not a good situation for follow-up movements.

ii Some boys will extend their out-turned foot to the ball far too late; it will then rebound away out of control.

The boy must offer his foot to the approaching ball and withdraw it as soon as the ball contacts the inside of the foot. The withdrawal of the relaxed leg and foot takes the pace off ('cushions') the ball. The faster the approaching ball the quicker the withdrawal must be. It may be useful for the boys to exaggerate this action so that the ball is held ('cushioned') longer than is really necessary.

iii Some boys will offer their foot to the ball at the correct time but will hold it there instead of withdrawing it; again, the

59

25 (above left). Foot extended to the ball.

26 (above right). Foot is withdrawn.

27 Ball still 'alive' just in front of the player.

ball will rebound against the rigid surface and control will be lost.

iv Some boys will withdraw their foot too far so that the ball comes to rest directly underneath them.

It should finish up just in front of the player and be still moving slightly so that the player can move off easily with an 'alive' ball.

v Most boys will control the ball with their better foot however it approaches them.

They should be encouraged to control the ball that approaches on their left side with their left foot and the ball coming to their right with their right foot. They will generally use their better foot to control the ball coming straight at them.

vi At this stage some boys will take their eyes off the ball.

They should watch the approaching ball on to the foot. As they become more skilful they should not need to watch the ball so closely.

Practice 2. (Ball between two boys)
As for the previous practice except that the ball is allowed to travel further so that the ball is brought under control as the body turns away from the original direction of travel of the ball. The body is then turned back and the ball returned to the partner who repeats the practice (Photos 28, 29, 30).

Common Faults—Corrections
All of the faults of the previous practice may occur.
In addition:

i The ball is controlled too early.

The ball must be controlled late enough to allow the player to turn as he controls it away from the original direction of travel of the ball.

28, 29 and 30. The foot is extended and the ball is brought under control as the body turns away from the original direction of travel of the ball.

Practice 3. (Ball between two boys)

The boys, still about 8–10 metres apart, now pass the ball to each other as they move anywhere in the playing area. They control and turn the ball with the inside of the foot, move off with it under control, and return it when they see the opportunity.

Common Faults—Corrections

It is much more difficult for boys to control a ball when they are on the move and the faults noted in the previous practice will be magnified. The importance of controlling the ball so that it remains 'alive', slightly in front of the boy, becomes more apparent in this practice.

i Because the boys are moving anywhere in the playing area they will encounter other boys.

They should control the ball away from this 'opposition'.

ii Some boys will return a pass regardless of the whereabouts of other boys.

They should retain the ball until a successful pass can be made. Even at this early stage boys should be encouraged to observe intelligently the movements of other players and make decisions accordingly.

(b) Small Group Practices with Opposition

At first only about half of the SKILL section of the lesson will be devoted to this type of work, but as the boys become more skilful it will take up a greater proportion of time until practices without opposition are dropped entirely. It is time to move on to the next aspect of CONTROL when the boys are reasonably proficient in this competitive situation.

The method of organising the small-group practices is modified slightly (Diagram 10). The number in each group remains the same

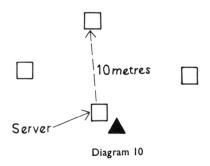

Diagram 10

as in the final stages of Passing, i.e. 4 *v*. 1. Now, however, one of the four passes the ball along the ground to any one of his colleagues, who should be about ten yards away. The one opponent stands beside the server and moves in to challenge the receiver as soon as the pass is made. When the receiver controls the ball he begins a passing movement with the other three and the opponent tries to intercept. After six consecutive passes have been made, or when the opponent gets the ball, the practice is repeated, the ball being served by whoever has the ball. As the receivers become more skilful the distance between the server and the receiver can be reduced to about seven yards.

Common Faults—Corrections

The faults already described in the practices without opposition will occur more frequently because of the presence of opposition. It is particularly important at this stage to:

i Control and turn the ball out of the path of the approaching opponent.

ii Decide quickly whether to control the ball or whether to pass it first time. Although the boys are concentrating on control at this stage, the teacher should insist that their passing is accurate. If an opponent has made a quick challenge there may not be time to control the ball. A first-time pass will, almost certainly, be more appropriate. The boys must assess the situation for themselves and make their decisions quickly.

USING THE INSIDE OF THE FOOT TO TAKE THE PACE OFF THE LOW BOUNCING BALL

(a) Practice of Techniques without Opposition

Practice 1. (Ball between two boys about 8–10 metres apart)
The boys serve the ball to each other with a two-handed underarm throw, so that it bounces below knee height. They control and turn the ball with the inside of the foot and return it along the ground (Photo 31).

Common Faults—Corrections

Most of the faults of the practice with the ball rolling along the ground will occur and should be corrected.

Practice 2. (Ball between two boys)
The boys, still about 8–10 metres apart, throw the ball to each other as they move about the playing area. They control and turn the ball with the inside of the foot, keep moving with it under control, and throw it back when they see an opportunity.

Common Faults—Corrections
As for Practice 2 of the previous technique.

31. Eyes on the ball as low bouncing ball is controlled.

Practice 3

As for Practice 2 except that the boy with the ball either serves a low bouncing ball or plays it with the foot along the ground.

Common Faults—Corrections

The receiver makes the wrong decision about which type of control to use.

An increase in the distance between the server and receiver will give the latter more time to make a decision.

(b) Small Group Practices with Opposition

The method of organisation is the same as for the previous practice with opposition. At first the server will only serve low bouncing balls so that the receiver need only concentrate on this type of control. When the boys are reasonably proficient either a ball rolling along the ground or a low bouncing ball is served. The receiver has to decide quickly which type of control to use.

Again, the distance between the server and the receiver can be reduced as skill increases, and the receiver may have to decide to pass the ball first time instead of controlling it. The boys are being put into progressively difficult situations in which decisions must be quickly made. This is the essence of these practices with opposition.

Common Faults—Corrections
The faults described in the practice without opposition will occur more frequently. It is also important as in the previous practice to:

i   Control the ball out of the path of an approaching opponent, by turning the ball with the controlling part of the body.

ii Decide quickly whether to control the ball or pass it first time.

iii When *either* a ball rolling along the ground or a low bouncing ball is served, another fault may occur. The receiver may have trouble in deciding which type of control to use for a particular service. This can only be corrected by a lot of practice and help from the teacher.

USING THE LOWER PART OF THE CHEST OR ABDOMEN TO TAKE THE PACE OFF THE HIGHER BOUNCING BALL

(a) Practice of Techniques without Opposition

Practice 1. (Ball between two boys about 5–6 metres apart)
The boys serve the ball to each other so that it rises fairly steeply after bouncing. The two-handed basketball bounce pass is used (Photos 32 and 33).

32. Well positioned to receive the higher bouncing ball.

33. Lower chest and abdomen are withdrawn and body arched over the ball so that it drops in front of him.

Common Faults—Corrections

i The receiver does not get in line with the approaching ball.

He should get his body quickly into line and be well balanced on both feet, with arms raised sideways when the ball arrives.

ii The lower chest or abdomen is not withdrawn quickly as the ball makes contact.

He must withdraw his lower chest and abdomen if the pace is to be taken off the ball.

iii The upper body is not arched over the ball.

He must arch and, at the same time, rotate his body to redirect the ball to the ground away from the line of the ball (Photos 34 and 35).

34 and 35. The body is arched and rotated to control and redirect the ball away from the original line of travel.

Practice 2. (Ball between two boys 5–6 metres apart)
The boys vary the type of service so that any of the three types of control already dealt with are practised.

Common Faults—Corrections
  i The receiver again makes the wrong decision about which type of control to use.

   An increase in the distance between the server and receiver will help, but regular practice is the key to further progress.

 ii The body is not rotated as contact is made with the ball. This must be done so that the player can move off in a different direction.

(b) Small Group Practices with Opposition

The method of organisation remains the same but the server and receiver begin the practice only 5–6 metres apart. At first the server will only serve the two-handed basketball bounce pass so that the receiver can concentrate on this type of control. When the boys are reasonably proficient any of the three types of service is used, i.e. a ball rolling along the ground, a low bouncing ball, or a higher bouncing ball. The receiver now has to decide which of *three* types of control is appropriate to the ball served to him with the added problem of opposition.

Common Faults—Corrections
The faults described in the practice without opposition will occur more frequently. As in the previous practice it is important to:
  i Control and turn the ball out of the path of an approaching opponent.
 ii Decide quickly whether to control the ball or pass it first time.
iii Decide which of the *three* types of control is appropriate.

36. Thigh offered to the dropping ball; boy well balanced. 37. Thigh lowered as ball makes contact. 38. Ball drops to the ground within easy controlling distance.

USING THE THIGH
TO TAKE THE PACE OFF A DROPPING BALL

This type of control is used when a ball is too low to control with the chest and too high to control with the foot (Photos 36–38).

(a) Practice of Techniques without Opposition

Practice 1. (Ball between two boys about 5 metres apart)
The boys lob the ball gently to each other so that it can be controlled on the thigh; an underarm lob is used.

Common Faults—Corrections

i The thigh is not lifted high enough towards the dropping ball.

It should be approximately at right angles to the line of the ball when contact is made.

ii The thigh is not lowered as the ball makes contact.

It should be lowered so that the ball drops gently on to the ground within easy controlling distance of the feet.

iii The thigh is not offered to the ball early enough and is still moving upwards when contact is made.

The boys should make an early upward movement so that the thigh is in position when the ball arrives.

iv Occasionally the thigh is held too high so that the ball rebounds towards the chest rather than dropping gently to the ground.

v The arms are not extended to assist balance.

Because the technique is performed while the boy is balanced on one leg, use of the arms is essential to assist balance.

vi The ball is not turned away from the line of flight.

Practice 2. (Ball between two boys)
The boys, about 5 metres apart, run anywhere in the playing area. One boy lobs the ball gently to his partner, who controls and turns it with the thigh, and moves away with the ball at his feet. He picks up the ball and lobs it to his partner who repeats the technique. The server varies the direction and trajectory of the lob.

Practice 3. (Ball between two boys)
As for Practice 2, except that the serve is varied so that any of the former types of control are practised.

Common Faults—Corrections
Again, the choice of the wrong type of control for the service will be the most common fault. The faults already noted in Practice 1 are likely to occur and should be corrected. Because boys are now on the move they will find the techniques more difficult to master; quick assessment of the type of service and movement into a position to receive it are essential. They must, of course, control and turn the ball away from other boys in the vicinity.

(a) Small Group Practice with Opposition

The method of organisation remains the same with the server and receiver only about 5–6 metres apart. At first only the lob on the thigh is used so that the receiver can concentrate on control with the thigh. When the boys are reasonably proficient the other three types of service are introduced so that the receiver has to decide which of *four* types of control is appropriate.

Common Faults—Corrections

The faults described in the practices without opposition will occur more frequently. As in the previous practices it is important to:

i   Decide quickly whether to control or pass the ball.

ii Decide which of *four* types of control is appropriate.

iii Control and turn the ball away from an approaching opponent (Photos 39, 40, 41).

iv Control the ball quickly if the opponent is very close (5–6 metres) and is likely to make a successful tackle.

39, 40 and 41. The thigh is offered to the dropping ball which is then controlled away from the original line of travel by lowering the thigh and turning the whole body.

USING THE CHEST
TO TAKE THE PACE OFF A DROPPING BALL

(b) Practice of Techniques without Opposition

Practice 1. (Ball between two boys about 5 metres apart)
The boys lob the ball gently to each other so that it can be controlled on the chest; a two-handed underarm throw is used and the trajectory increased gradually (Photo 42).

42. The body in position for controlling the ball with the chest.

Common Faults—Corrections
i The chest is not withdrawn as the ball hits it.

In all the types of control dealt with in this chapter, the receiving surface must be withdrawn along the line of the approaching ball and then, as the ball makes contact, rotated so that the ball is moved away from the line of flight.

ii The knees are not bent and the body arched backwards to allow the line of the ball to be approximately at right angles to the chest.

The extent to which the knees are bent and the body arched will depend on the trajectory of the ball. The steeper the trajectory the more pronounced the bending and the arching must be.

iii The arms are not extended properly.

They must, of course, be extended to assist balance, but in this technique they have a further important role. They are held at about shoulder height and forwards as well as outwards, as if hugging a very fat person. This means that the more fleshy parts of the chest are drawn together to present a soft surface to the ball. If they are held sideways a very rigid surface will be presented to the ball. If, however, they are held too low, and close together, there is a chance that the receiver will be penalised for handling the ball.

Practice 2. (Ball between two boys about 5 metres apart)
The boys run anywhere in the playing area. One boy lobs the ball gently to his partner, who controls and turns it with his chest and moves away with the ball at his feet. He picks the ball up and lobs it to his partner who repeats the technique. The server varies the trajectory of the lob.

Common Faults—Corrections
The faults already noted in Practice 1 are likely to occur and should be corrected. Quick assessment of type of service and movement into a position to control it are again essential. The ball must again be controlled and turned away from other boys in the immediate vicinity: this is done by turning the top half of the body towards the free space into which the ball is to be directed just as contact is made (Photos 43, 44, 45).

Practice 3. (Ball between two boys)
As for Practice 2 except that the serve is varied so that any of the four types of control are practised.

43, 44 and 45. The chest is offered to the steeply dropping ball and then controlled away from the original line of travel by withdrawing the chest and turning the whole body at the same time.

Common Faults—Corrections

Again, the use of the wrong type of control for the service.

(b) Small Group Practice with Opposition

The method of organisation remains the same, with the server about 5–6 metres away from the receiver. At first only the high two-handed lob is used, so that the boys can master this comparatively difficult technique. When the boys are reasonably skilful the other four types of service are introduced, so that the receiver has to decide which of *five* types of control to use, again with the added problem of opposition.

Common Faults—Corrections

The faults described in the practices without opposition will be more common. As in all these practices it is important to:

i Control and turn the ball away from an approaching opponent.

ii Decide quickly whether to control or pass the ball.

iii Decide which of *five* types of control to use.

iv Control pass the ball quickly as the opponent is very near.

There is no reason why the head should not be used to pass or even control the ball if it is too high for the chest. Skilful boys will do this instinctively.

At this stage the boys should be quite skilful and the teacher should stress that they should use the technique that will get the ball under control quickly rather than waiting for the ball to arrive in order to use the technique they find easiest.

7: Basic Tactics

All of the teaching of this topic is done through small group practices with opposition in groups of 3 *v*. 1. If, however, the practices are failing because of poor passing, the teacher might include some passing practices without opposition at the beginning of the SKILL TRAINING (Chapter 5) part of the lesson.

MOVEMENT OFF THE BALL

Practice 1. (3 *v*. 1)
The three boys, using a basketball chest pass, try to prevent the opponent intercepting the ball. A basketball chest pass is used at this stage, as it is easier to bring out the teaching points. The groups should work in a restricted area, i.e. ten metres square.

If the opponent is to be prevented from intercepting the ball, the movement of the two boys without the ball is crucial. They should move into positions on either side of the opponent so that the boy in possession has two definite passing possibilities. In effect the three boys form a wide triangle with the opponent in the centre.

As the three boys pass the ball amongst themselves, the triangular formation is adjusting and re-adjusting to give the boy in possession the two passing opportunities. For example (Diagram 11), if player A passes the ball to player B, player C will have to move quickly from C1 to C2 so that player B, now in possession, has the two passing opportunities.

The boys should always be aware of their own positions in relation to where the ball and the opponent are.

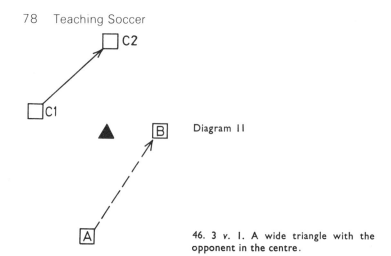

Diagram II

46. 3 v. I. A wide triangle with the opponent in the centre.

Common Faults—Corrections

i One of the three boys, C, stands too close to the opponent Diagram 11).

There is still a triangle but it is not a wide one. Player B's

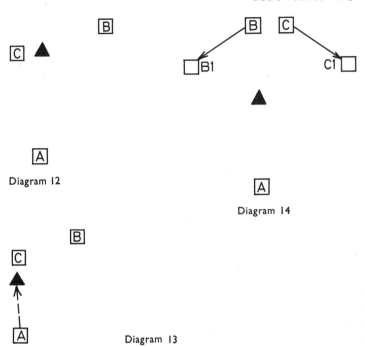

Diagram 12

Diagram 14

Diagram 13

pass is quite likely to be intercepted. The boys must be encouraged to keep well away from the opponents.

ii One of the boys, C, stands behind the opponent (Diagram 13).

One of the passing possibilities has been eliminated. As the boys are restricted to basketball chest passes, they cannot direct the pass over the opponent.

The boys should *never* get themselves into this 'hiding' position.

iii Both boys not in possession are caught behind the opponent (Diagram 14 Photo 47).

Player A has little chance of making a successful pass to either player.

47. 3 v. 1. Both opponents caught behind the opponent (page 79).

Players B and C must move to positions B1 and C1 to form the side triangle that allows the two passing possibilities.

The boys should avoid such crowding at all costs.

Practice 2

As for Practice 1 except that the boys now pass the ball with the feet (e.g. Photo 46).

The same faults will occur as in the previous practice. The practice will break down more regularly as it is far more difficult to both control and pass the ball with the feet.

Although this practice will gradually take over the bulk of the SKILL TRAINING part of the lesson, it should always be preceded, if only briefly, by the practice using the basketball chest pass, so that the teaching points can be emphasised in a comparatively simple situation.

A high standard of passing and control is necessary if this practice is to be successful and the teacher should not hesitate to repeat some of the practices from Chapters 5 and 6 if he feels that faulty passing and control are causing the practice to break down.

CALLING INSTRUCTIONS

As the boys improve in their movement off the ball, they should be encouraged to help each other by calling helpful instructions.

Calling instructions during practice and team play is a skill of the game and, if properly used, can be highly effective. Like everything else, it must be practised, even by goalkeepers.

At first many boys will find it difficult to talk to each other during practice, apart, of course, from irrelevant chatter, which should be eliminated from the start. If they are given a few simple instructions that can be repeated many times during a practice their confidence in intelligent, relevant calling will increase.

1. 'HOLD'

This call should be made by the passer to the boy receiving the ball if the opponent is some distance away, and not therefore likely to make a tackle. Of course, the receiver may be fully aware that the opponent is not within tackling distance, but there are occasions when he isn't and must rely upon the quick relevant calls of the passer.

2. 'PASS'

This call should be made by colleagues of the boy receiving the ball who, under pressure from the opponent, hasn't time or space to bring the ball under control. The receiver should try and be aware of the situation himself, but the intelligent calls of his colleagues will give him a double check on deciding whether to control or pass the ball.

3. ASKING FOR A PASS

Boys are more willing to call for a pass, as they like to be in possession of the ball. They must, however, learn *when* to make the call. The call is only made when the caller is in, or moving into, a position where he can be reached by a simple pass; in other words when he is in a supporting position to the boy in possession.

Again, the boy in possession should have summed up the situation for himself, and seen his colleagues move into good supporting positions, but the calls of his colleagues will give him a double check. Occasionally, he may not be aware of the position of his colleagues; intelligent calling from them in this situation is vital.

The boys should get into the habit of calling the name of the boy in possession when they want a pass, as anything else may earn the disapproval of the referee.

Common Faults—Corrections

i Boys will often shout continuously to attract the attention of the boy in possession.

They should call only when they are in a good position to receive the ball.

The boy in possession will tend to ignore the boy who calls for the ball when he is covered by an opponent. The opponent will also know where he is!

ii Boys will often make vague purposeless calls, such as 'Get rid of it', 'Kick it'.

All calls must be simple and have a clear purpose.

MOVEMENT WITH THE BALL

At this stage the boys should be skilful enough for the teacher to encourage a positive attitude towards the opponent.

Practice 1. (3 *v*. 1)

In previous practices of this type, the player in possession will have waited for the opponent to make a challenge before he passed the ball. Now he takes the initiative by taking the ball towards the space immediately to the left or right of the challenging player. He makes his pass, or dribbles past the opponent, as he commits himself to a tackle (Photos 48 and 49). Having made

48. 3 *v.* 1. Boy in possession takes the ball to the opponent.

49. 3 *v.* 1. Dribbles past him as challenge is made.

the pass, the boy carries on with his run into a position where he is in a good supporting position to the new man in possession. The new man in possession must, in his turn, decide whether to attack the opponent's space or make a first-time pass. If the opponent has been beaten it should be unnecessary to make a first-time pass. This practice is confined to an area approximately ten yards square.

Common Faults—Corrections

i The supporting players do not move quickly into position to maintain the wide triangle with the opponent in the middle.

The whole pattern of movement will be faster as the boy in possession is moving quickly into space on either side of the challenger and unless his colleagues are reacting as quickly he will be in trouble.

ii The boy in possession runs directly at the opponent. He should attack the spaces on either side of the challenger and then pass or beat him, using his dribbling skills.

iii The boy in possession does not keep the ball closely under control.

He must keep it under control if he is to pass the ball either way at the last possible moment.

iv The boy in possession uses the wrong passing technique. If the ball is to be sent to the left, either the inside of the right foot or the outside of the left foot should be used. If the ball is to be passed to the right, either the inside of the left or the outside of the right should be used.

In this 'tight' situation, the most effective pass will often be the one with the outside of the foot, as it can be made quickly and allows the passer to continue his run past the opponent more easily (Chapter 5, The Pass with the Outside of the Foot).

At first the boys will only be able to concentrate on one aspect of this topic at a time but with practice they will, as a matter of habit, move in to sound supporting positions, call intelligently and make runs with the ball towards the spaces alongside the challenger.

Practice 2. (3 *v.* 1) (The Wall Pass)
The practice is exactly the same as the previous one except that the boys try to beat the opponent by using 'the wall pass' whenever possible.

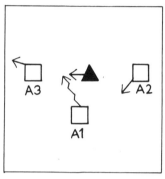

Diagram 15

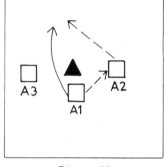

Diagram 16

A1 runs with the ball towards the space alongside the opponent in order to pull him in that direction. As A1 moves in this direction, A2 moves to offer close support. As this movement is happening, A3, seeing that he is not being used in this piece of play, moves away from the area to give more space to A1 and A2 (diagram 15). When A1 is quite close to the challenger he passes the ball softly to A2 and immediately runs round the other side of the challenger to receive a first-time pass from A2 (diagram 16). This is 'the wall pass'. (Photos 50 and 51).

Common Faults—Corrections
   i A1, because he is too anxious to beat the opponent, hits the ball too firmly to A2 who has difficulty passing it back accurately to A1 as he makes his run into the new position.

50. The player with the ball, when challenged, passes it to a colleague.

51. He then runs round the other side of the challenger to receive a first-time pass.

The ball should be played 'softly' enough to allow A1 to return it accurately.

ii A1 plays the ball with the inside of the left foot and thus puts himself in an awkward crossed-legged position before he makes his run.

He should pass the ball with the outside of his right foot and so be nicely balanced to sprint past the challenger to receive the return pass.

8: Heading

HEADING THE BALL FORWARD, FROM A STANDING POSITION

(a) Practice of Techniques without Opposition

Practice 1. (Ball between two boys about 5 metres apart)
The boy with the ball holds it in front of him at head height.
He heads it out of his hands to his partner, who controls it with a
suitable technique before heading the ball back in the same way
(Photos 52–54).

Faults to look for

i The ball is not struck with the forehead.

When the header is made the head and top part of the body
should be directed at the ball so that the middle of the forehead, the ball and target are all in line.

ii The ball is brought back to the forehead.

The reverse should happen. The head and top part of the
body are first withdrawn and then thrust forward so that the
forehead meets the ball with some force. The ball should
never be brought back towards the head.

iii The eyes are closed.

They must be kept open so that the ball can be lined up and
headed in the right direction with the middle of the forehead.

iv The feet are set astride.

They should be placed one in front of the other, otherwise
quite a lot of power will be lost. In this position a greater

87

52. The head and upper body are withdrawn (page 87).

53. The ball is hit with the forehead (page 87).

54. The header is made with both feet still on the ground (page 87).

55. The ball is thrown up in front of the head (page 90).

56. The timing is correct and the ball is headed downwards with the forehead (page 90).

range of movement is possible resulting in a more powerful header.

v The body is thrown at the ball with both feet off the ground.

Again, power is lost and the header is likely to be inaccurate. The feet must be kept on the ground.

Practice 2. (Ball between two boys about 5 metres apart)
The boy in possession now throws the ball a few feet above and just in front of his head. He heads it to his partner from a standing position. His partner controls it and returns it in the same way (Photos 55 and 56).

Faults to look for

i The timing of the header is faulty.

The top part of the body must be withdrawn and then thrust forward so that the forehead meets the dropping ball. If the thrust forward is made too early the dropping ball will hit him high on the head; if, however, the thrust is made too late, the ball will be contacted with the nose, mouth or chin, which will be both inaccurate and uncomfortable. Correct timing can only be achieved through regular practice.

ii The eyes are closed or not kept on the ball.

As timing is crucial in this technique, the boys must watch the ball carefully.

Practice 3. (Ball between two boys about 5 metres apart)
The boy in possession serves the ball with an underhand throw so that his partner can head it back without jumping. Each boy serves ten and heads ten balls.

Faults to look for
The common faults have been described in Practices 1 and 2. In this practice the receiver will have to adjust his return header according to the type of service he receives.

(b) Small Group Practices with Opposition

The groups remain at the 3 *v.* 1 level as in the previous topic. The server, about 5–6 metres from the receiver, serves the ball with an underhand throw to any one of his colleagues so that he can return it with his head without jumping. The three then try to make six consecutive passes with their feet. When they have done that, or when the opponent gets the ball, the practice is repeated, the ball being served by whoever is in possession of the ball. The practice continues until each boy has been both an opponent and a receiver.

In the early stages the opponent should be positioned some distance from both the server and the receiver (8–10 yards) so that his challenge cannot be made too quickly. As heading ability increases the distance can be decreased (Diagram 17).

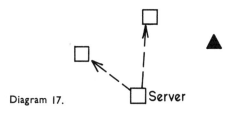

Diagram 17.   Server

Common Faults—Corrections

The faults of the previous practice will occur more readily because an opponent has been introduced. In addition, the boys will not fully appreciate that the header back to the server is a pass, even though it is made with the head.

i The header is not accurate and the receiver has to move to control it.

ii The power of the header is not judged correctly.

  The boy must learn to judge the effort he puts into it, according to the distance the receiver and the opponent are away.

iii The ball does not reach the receiver at a controllable height.

Ideally it should be directed to the feet so that control of it can be gained quickly.

iv After heading the ball the boy doesn't move immediately into a supporting position so that the consecutive passing movement with the feet can be started successfully.

He shouldn't watch his header being controlled before he moves. Quick movement in support is essential, particularly when the opponent is moved in closer to challenge. The receiver should find his colleagues in good supporting positions when he has the decision to make whether to control the ball or pass it first time.

HEADING THE BALL FORWARD FROM A JUMP

(a) Practice of Techniques without Opposition

Practice 1

The boy with the ball takes a couple of strides and jumps to head it from his hands to his partner; he controls it and heads it back in the same way. The jump can be made from one or two feet, though the former is probably more efficient.

Common Faults—Corrections

Many of the faults of the standing header will occur; in addition:

i The jump will be made directly underneath the ball and it will strike the upturned forehead or the top of the head.

The ball must be held slightly in front of the head so that the upper body and head can be thrust forward at it.

Practice 2. (Ball between two boys, 7–8 metres apart)

The boy in possession now throws the ball higher and further in front of him. He takes a stride or two and jumps to head the ball to his partner, who controls it and returns it in the same way. The jump can be made from one or two feet, though the former is probably the more efficient.

Common Faults—Corrections
Fault (i) of the previous practice is most likely to occur again. In addition:

i The jump is not timed correctly. Many boys will jump too early and will either miss the ball entirely or just reach it with the top of their heads. In the early stages boys should be encouraged to wait for the ball to fall before they stride forward and jump to head it.

   As timing improves the boys should try to meet the ball at a higher point in the air until they are eventually meeting it at maximum jumping height. This is a complex body movement when performed in the air and the boys should be taught it in careful stages. At first they need only jump to let the ball hit the forehead, but gradually they can be encouraged to withdraw the head and eventually the whole upper body.

Practice 3. (Ball between two boys, 7–8 metres apart)
The boy in possession serves the ball with an underhand throw so that his partner has to take a couple of strides and jump to return it with a header. Each boy serves ten and heads ten back.

Common Faults—Corrections
The common faults have already been described in Practices 1 and 2. In this practice the receiver will have to adjust his jump and header according to the type of serve he receives. In fact, as skill increases, the server should be encouraged to vary the serve slightly.

Practice 4. (3 *v.* 1)

(b) Small Group Practices with Opposition

The organisation is the same as for the previous small group practice, but now the ball is served a little higher, so that the receiver has to jump to head it.

Common Faults—Corrections
The faults of the small group work for the standing header

will occur more readily because an opponent has been introduced. The opponent will, of course, be some distance away and will be unable to make a quick challenge, but until the boys acquire skill at this very difficult technique, they will not have a lot of time to head the ball accurately before a challenge is made. The technique only develops slowly but many boys will eventually reach a level of skill that gives them time to perform the technique with apparent care and lack of haste, even when closely challenged.

HEADING THE BALL FORWARD FROM EITHER A STANDING POSITION OR A JUMP

(a) Practice of Techniques without Opposition

Practice 1. (Ball between two boys about five metres apart)
One boy serves the ball with an underhand lob to his partner who heads it back. The server varies the height of the lob so that his partner must decide whether to jump for it or head it from a standing position. The headers must be returned directly to the server (preferably to his feet), who controls it and repeats the service. After ten services the roles are reversed.

Faults to look for
Many of the faults of the previous practices will occur. In addition:

The receiver will not decide quickly enough to jump for the ball served with a higher trajectory.

He must decide early otherwise he won't be in a good position to head the ball properly.

(b) Small Group Practices with Opposition

The organisation is the same as for the previous small group practices but now the server varies his serves. Some are low, so that the receiver need not jump; others are served so that a jump is necessary. The receiver has to assess each serve and use the appropriate technique.

Common Faults—Corrections

Many of the faults of the previous practices will occur. It is particularly important in this competitive situation that the boy decides quickly whether or not he has to jump for the ball. It must be stressed that throughout the small group practices, once the header has been made, the teacher should be encouraging a high standard of skill in the topics already taught—passing, control and basic tactics.

THE ANGLED HEADER
FROM THE STANDING POSITION

This is a more difficult technique than the forward header, but older boys and the more skilful younger ones, are quite capable of mastering it.

(a) Practice of Techniques without Opposition

Practice 1. (Ball between three boys)
The boys stand in a triangular formation about five metres apart. One boy serves the ball slightly to the side of a colleague, with an underarm throw, so that it can be headed sideways from a standing position to the third player (Photo 57). He controls it and serves it to the previous server who heads it sideways to the first performer. The practice continues until each player has had several headers in one direction; practice is then reversed so that the boys get practice in heading the ball in the other direction.

Faults to look for
i The ball is hit with the side of the head. This is caused by the boy thrusting his head sideways to contact the ball, on the side of the forehead at best, but possibly on the temple or ear; this can be uncomfortable, and even dangerous, and is rarely accurate.
  The boy must watch the ball carefully and as it is served, rotate his upper body so that the forehead is facing the intended target. The body is thus thrust towards the target so that the middle of the forehead contacts the ball.

57. The upper body is rotated so that the ball can be headed sideways with the forehead (page 95).

ii Timing is faulty.

The thrust towards the target must be timed so that the middle of the forehead guides the ball to the third boy. This can only be achieved if the performer watches the ball carefully. He should first concentrate on timing and add power later.

iii The back foot is not moved.

As the ball approaches it should move backwards so that the

stance is comfortable and the upper body can lean backwards more easily.

Practice 2. (Ball between two boys)
The organisation is the same as for the previous practice except that the service is directed straight at the receiver who heads it sideways to the third player.

Common Faults—Corrections
As for the previous practice. In addition:

i The rotation of the upper body and lean backwards does not take the forehead outside the line of flight of the ball.

As the ball is now being thrown straight at the boy heading it, he must move his upper body out of the line of flight and rotate it so it can be thrust towards the target.

(b) Small Group Practice with Opposition

The organisation remains the same (3 *v.* 1). The boy heading the ball can decide, according to the type of service he receives, whether he heads the ball forward or sideways. Again he is in a situation demanding the making of decisions.

THE ANGLED HEADER FROM A JUMP

(a) Practice of Techniques without Opposition

Practice 1. (Ball between three boys)
The organisation is the same as for the previous practice without opposition, but the ball is served so that the receiver has to jump to head it sideways. At this stage the serve is directed slightly to the side of the receiver so that he can head it sideways more easily (Photo 58).

Common Faults—Corrections
Faults (i) and (ii) of the angled header from a standing position will be likely to occur. Timing is the essence of this practice,

58. The ball is headed sideways from a jump (page 97).

because the performer is not only concerned with directing the ball sideways but also in jumping for it.

iii The jump is made too early. In this case the boy will either miss the ball entirely or it will merely strike him on the top or side of his head.

iv The jump is made too late. If contact is made it will not be with the forehead and there will be no time to direct the ball in the required direction.

Both of these are faults of timing and can only be corrected by regular practice and by watching the flight of the ball very carefully.

Practice 2. (Ball between three boys)
The organisation is the same as for the previous practice, but now the ball is thrown straight at the receiver who must jump and head it sideways.

Common Faults—Corrections
As for the previous practice. In addition:
v The rotation of the upper body and lean backwards does not take the forehead outside the line of flight of the ball.

The combination of a jump, rotation of the upper body, leaning backwards and moving the forehead outside the line of flight is a complex movement, and will need plenty of practice.

(b) Small Group Practices with Opposition

The organisation remains the same (3 *v.* 1) but now the service is raised so that the receiver is put into a situation where he has to decide which of the four types of header is appropriate to the situation. For example, if the challenger anticipates a header back to the server, it can be directed sideways.

DEFENSIVE HEADING

Up to this point the stress has been on attacking heading, i.e. heading the ball downwards towards the goal or to the feet of a supporting player. The boys can now be introduced to the technique of defensive heading, i.e. heading the ball upwards away from opponents in the goal area.

The difference in technique from the attacking header is minimal. In order to give height to the ball it must be struck slightly lower down than for the attacking header.

(a) Practice of Techniques without Opposition

Practice 1. (Ball between three boys)
The boys stand in a line about five metres apart. The centre boy serves the ball, with an underarm throw, to one of his colleagues

59. The ball is headed over the top of the server to the third player.

60. The ball should be struck just below the centre so that it clears the server.

who heads it over the top of the server to the third player who controls and turns it before returning it to the server. The practice continues with each player taking his turn as a server (Photo 59).

Common Faults—Corrections

As for all the previous practices. In addition:

i The ball is struck too high so that it is directed downwards towards the server.

ii The ball is struck too low so that it goes straight up in the air.

The ball should be struck just below the centre so that it is given sufficient height to clear the server (Photo 60).

(b) Small Group Practices with Opposition

The organisation remains the same (3 *v.* 1) as for previous practices but now the receiver can either head the ball downwards to a colleague or over the top of the server to a colleague already in position some distance away. He can, of course, also head the ball into a space for a colleague to move into and receive.

9: Challenging, Dribbling and Movement with and without the Ball

THE BASIC TACKLE

This tackle is used when a player with the ball under close control moves directly at the challenger who, in order to make a successful challenge, blocks the movement of the ball with the inside of his tackling foot.

(a) Practice of Techniques without Opposition

Practice 1. (Ball between two boys)
The ball is placed on the ground between the two players so that each make one stride to challenge for it. At a signal from the teacher or one of the players they each take a stride forward and block the ball with the inside of the same foot (Photos 61 and 62).

Faults to look for
i The non-tackling foot is not placed firmly on the ground alongside the ball with toe pointing forward.

ii The upper body is leaning backwards.

The body should be leaning forward so that the boy is looking down at the ball.

iii The tackling foot is not turned sideways.

The inside of the foot should be presented to the ball as if making a pass with the inside of the foot. This is, of course, easier to achieve if the leg is bent slightly.

61. Non-tackling foot firmly on the ground alongside the ball, tackling foot thrust sideways and presented firmly to the ball; eyes on the ball.

62. The near boy has his non-tackling and tackling feet close together. The other boy is in a bad tackling position.

iv The tackling foot is not presented firmly to the ball and will be pushed aside.

Although the weight of the body must remain on the non-tackling foot, the tackling foot must be firm.

v There is a gap between the tackling and non-tackling feet.

These should be as close together as possible forming a right angle through which the ball cannot be forced.

vi The ball is not struck in the centre. If it is struck too high the ball can be pushed underneath the foot; if it is struck too low the ball can be forced over the top.

The inside of the foot must meet the ball firmly in the centre.

Practice 2. (One ball between two boys)
One boy dribbles the ball, closely under control, towards the space on either side of his partner who tries to make a successful tackle. If he wins the ball he turns and dribbles towards his dispossessed partner, who becomes the challenger.

Faults to look for
The faults described in the previous practice will occur more readily because the dribbler has forward momentum. In addition:

vii The challenger stands flatfooted as he prepares to make his tackle.

He should crouch slightly, and be up on his toes. This position of alertness is essential if the challenger is to be prepared for any evasive movements the dribbler will make later (Photo 63).

Practice 3. (One ball between two boys)
The organisation is the same as for the previous practice except that the boy with the ball has a target. He starts from a line and his object is to reach a line fifteen to twenty yards away without being tackled. If he is successful he will attempt to make the return

journey without being tackled. If the challenger wins the ball he takes it to the line from which the other boy started, and the practice continues. The dribbler must, of course, use the dribbling

63. The challenger is in a good position, slightly crouched and on his toes (page 104).

skills he has been practising in the introductory part of the lesson, to beat his partner, always attacking the spaces on either side of his opponent.

Faults to look for
The faults of the previous practices will occur. In addition:

i The challenger is tempted to 'dive' into the tackle.

   He should be patient and retreat slowly, allowing the dribbler to get close enough to make a tackle possible.

ii He faces the opponent squarely.

   His body should be half turned, semi-crouched and slightly to one side of the opponent. By adopting this position he can force the dribbler to one side, rather than offering him two routes, and he is in a better position to recover if the attacker manages to get past him. In fact, the challenger is not allowing the attacker to dictate matters.

iii He exaggerates the half-turned position and is looking over his shoulder at the attacker. This will allow the attacker to go behind him and he is no longer dictating events.

(b) Small Group Practices with Opposition

The boys are in groups of 2 *v*. 1 and all work is done in narrow lanes or 'corridors' about twenty metres long and four to five metres wide (Photo 67). If the playground has been marked out as suggested in Chapter 3, it will be a simple matter to add the lines required (Diagram 18).

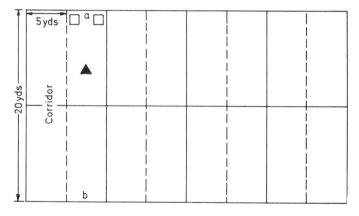

Diagram 18.

By chalking in the lines shown, eight corridors, twenty metres by five metres, are created.

The two attackers, starting from point (a), try to get past the challenger to point (b) by either passing or dribbling the ball. If they succeed they return in the opposite direction. If the ball goes outside the 'corridor' the practice must be restarted. If the challenger is successful he tries to get to the point from which the attackers have come.

The activity can be made really competitive by seeing which boy makes the most successful challenge in ten attacks.

Faults to look for

All of the faults of the previous practice will occur more readily. Now that there are two challengers it is particularly important that:

He does not 'dive' into the tackle. If he does it will be a simple matter for the two attackers to beat him.

He should retract slowly trying to delay the attackers. In fact if he is able to 'contain' them until he arrives at their target line, he will have achieved his purpose. In full-scale games one of the skills of the defender is to 'contain' attackers until he gets help from his colleagues. It is not enough, however, for him merely to retreat. He should be trying to reduce the distance between him and the player with the ball and forcing him into a position where he cannot pass the ball.

The success of this practice is also determined by the urgency of the attackers. They must not allow the defender to slow them down but must carry out all their movements quickly, whether dribbling or passing in order to put the defender under pressure.

DRIBBLING AND MOVEMENT WITH AND WITHOUT THE BALL

It is at this stage that the boys will have to refine their dribbling ability and basic tactics of movement with and without the ball in order to deceive challengers. All practices are done with opposition.

Practice 1. (2 *v.* 1)
The 'corridor' should now be about 10 metres wide to allow sufficient space for the two attackers to develop their skills but still

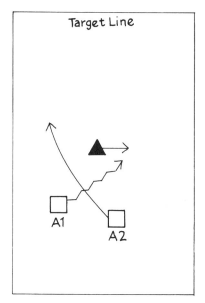

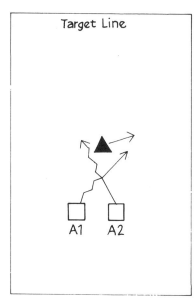

Diagram 19   Diagram 20

realistic enough for the challenger to put them under pressure. The practice is otherwise exactly the same as the previous one. The attackers can try various ways of beating the defender, e.g.

i A1 moves with the ball across the front of the defender. As the defender moves across to cut off the run, A2 runs into a forward position behind A1 and the defender (Diagram 19). A2 must, of course, time his run so that he does not get himself into what might be an off-side position in a real game.

ii (Diagram 20) A1 runs towards the defender controlling the ball with the foot furthest from the defender (right foot in this case). The defender moves across to cover the run but as A1 almost reaches the defender he leaves the ball and allows A2 to take it in the space left by the opponent. (Photos **64** and **65**.)

64 and 65. The player with the ball, when challenged, puts
his foot on it and leaves it for his colleague.

The transfer of the ball must be made at a point at which A1 is between A2 and the defender.

There are, of course, many other ways of beating the defender, and the two attackers, particularly the one with the ball, must be ready to use them.

The practice should continue until the attackers reach their target line or area. Many players attempt a movement or trick and if it is unsuccessful, give up. They must be encouraged to continue the practice until they are dispossessed or have found a way of beating the defender.

Practice 2 (4 *v.* 1).
The practice is the same as the previous one except that two further attackers (A3 and A4) are introduced. They cannot, however,

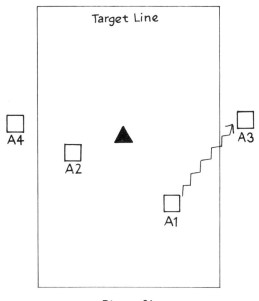

Diagram 21

66 and 67. The ball is 'screened' from the opponent, using the outside of the foot, and then passed to a colleague.

enter the 'corridor', but position themselves just on or outside the side-lines (Diagram 21).

A1 and A2 can now take the ball to either A3 or A4 when a transfer is attempted and the 2 *v*. 1 situation in the corridor is continued with either A3 or A4 replacing A1 or A2. The objective is still for A1 or A2 to reach the target line with the ball. This

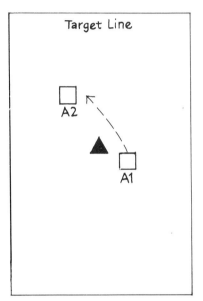

Diagram 22

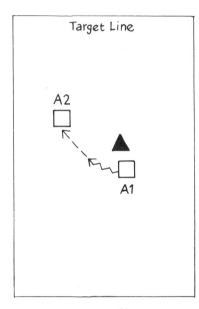

Diagram 23

practice will give the attackers the opportunity to use the full range of passing and dribbling skills they have developed to beat a challenge. It will be particularly useful in attempting 'the wall pass'.

A1 can, if space is available, pass immediately forward to A2 (Diagram 22). Or he can 'screen' the ball from the defender, by turning quickly, using the outside of his right foot and then passing to A2 (Diagram 23), (Photos 70 and 71).

10 : Shooting

Many of these practices require a wall or other rebound surface. This is where the old playgrounds are so useful (see pages 25-6). but rebound surfaces can be constructed in modern playgrounds. Such surfaces can, of course, be used for the teaching of the skills of many games.

(a) Practice of Techniques without Opposition
Practice 1. (Ball to each boy)
The boys stand about 10 metres away from a wall or other rebound surface and strike the ball against it using either foot. They control the rebounding ball before striking it again against the wall (Photo 68).

Common Faults—Corrections

  i The ball is hit too hard. This is a natural fault as the boys will associate shooting with power.

     At this stage the emphasis should be on striking the ball accurately and not on power.

  ii The ball is struck with the wrong part of the foot.
     It should be struck, whenever possible, with the upper surface of the boot; the laces part of the boot is a good description. This will promote a toes-down position of the foot (Photo 69). This foot position is absolutely crucial in shooting. Players will rarely have much time when they find themselves in scoring situations and they cannot think about the positioning of their non-kicking foot or the alignment of their bodies. If they do the scoring chance will have gone.

68. Striking the ball against a rebound surface, using either foot. Note toes-down position of the striking foot.

iii What they can, and should, do is concentrate solely on striking the ball with the laces part of the boot. If they do this they will have a reasonable degree of success at the most crucial skill in soccer; the ultimate aim, after all, is to score goals.

iv The player takes his eyes off the ball as he is kicking it. He should keep his eyes on the point of contact even after the ball has gone. (Photo 70).

v Only one foot is used. Players in shooting positions have no time to choose their best foot. They must be proficient with both and should be encouraged to use both in *all* shooting practices.

Practice 2. As for Practice 1 except that the boys now hit the ball first time as it rebounds from the wall. The aim is now to establish a rhythm.

69. Toes-down position of the foot when shooting.

70. The player keeps his eyes on the ball even after it has gone.

Common Faults—Corrections

The faults described in the previous practice will occur. In addition:

   i The rhythm is lost because the boys try to return a very difficult ball with the laces part of the boot. Although, whenever possible, the laces part of the boot should be used, there are occasions when a very difficult ball should be returned with the inside or outside of the foot or whatever part retains the rhythm of this practice.

Practice 3. As for Practice 2, but the distance from player to wall is reduced to 5 metres.

Common Faults—Correction

As for previous practice, but the rhythm of the practice now becomes all-important and although, whenever possible, the laces part of either boot should be used, the rhythm can only be maintained if any part is used.

Practice 4. (Ball between two boys about 8–10 metres from a rebound surface)

One boy strikes the ball against the wall, as in the previous practices and his partner attempts to hit the rebound first time against the wall. The practice is continued as long as possible.

Common Faults—Corrections

As for previous practices it is particularly important in this practice that the ball is hit accurately rather than powerfully so that the partner isn't faced with an unplayable return. This is a co-operative practice in which the players establish a rhythm which helps both.

As the players become more skilful they can hit the ball more powerfully. At this stage they will require a target on the wall (a goal) to limit their area of shooting.

Practice 5. As for the previous practice except that an area where two walls meet is used. This increases the difficulty and gets the boys used to hitting balls coming at them from different angles.

If rebound surfaces are not available the above practice can be done in pairs with the boys, about 8–10 metres apart, striking the ball to each other.

Practice 6. (Ball between two boys about 20 metres apart)

The pairs work in a marked area about 20 metres long and 10 metres wide and attempt to hit the ball round a skittle to each other. Players A and C will each have to use their left foot to swerve the ball round the skittle and players B and D their right feet. They can change over from time to time so that they practise with both feet. (See diagram p. 118.)

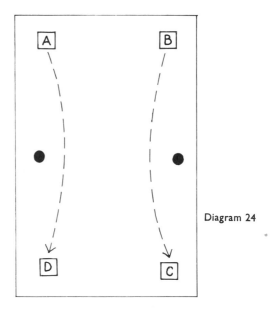

Diagram 24

● Skittles or cones

Common Faults—Correction

i The ball is hit in the vertical centre line of the ball. In this
practice the object is to swerve or 'bend' the ball in flight,
and contact should be made to one side of the centre line.

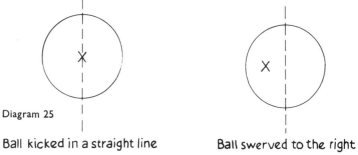

Diagram 25

Ball kicked in a straight line

Ball swerved to the right

This skill is utilised very often at free-kicks near goal to 'bend' a ball round a 'wall' of players, but it can also be used in any shooting situation to deceive the goalkeeper.

ii The ball is hit too hard.

At first the emphasis should be on accuracy but gradually power should be linked to swerve.

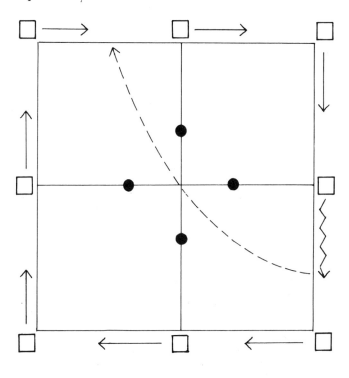

● Skittles or cones

Diagram 26

Practice 7. (Ball between 5–8 players using an area about 20 metres by 20 metres)

The players move round the perimeter of the area. When they receive the ball they control it before shooting it between the skittles, with or without swerve. As they become more skilful and confident they can try first-time shots.

Common Faults—Correction
As for all previous practices.

(b) Small Group Practices with Opposition

Practice 1. (Ball between 5 boys, one acting as goalkeeper)

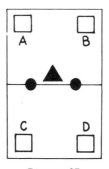

Diagram 27

Attackers A and B try to get the ball to attackers D and C by shooting the ball past the goalkeeper. The ball is hit first time whenever possible, even from the goalkeeper clearance. Each player takes a turn as goalkeeper.

Common Faults—Correction
As for all the previous practices.

Practice 2. (5 *v.* 3)
In restricted areas of the playground or field, the 5 try to score goals against the 3 (one acting as goalkeeper). The ball is cleared to the start line or returned there after a goal is scored.

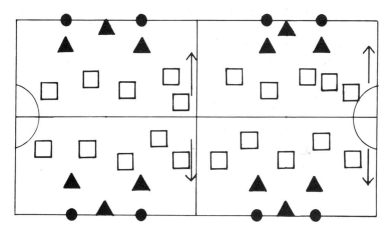

Diagram 28

Common Faults—Correction

All the faults of the previous practices. In addition:

There will be occasions when a player who is not in a good scoring position will shoot instead of passing to a colleague who *is* in a scoring position.

Players should be encouraged to look for colleagues in scoring positions though the maxim 'if in doubt shoot' is not a bad one.

11: Further Progress

The introduction of a second and a third opponent in the practices with opposition is the key to further progress, so that eventually the evenly balanced small-side game will be played with skill and understanding. The small group practices with opposition are repeated but the number of opponents is increased as follows:

$$5 \ v. \ 2$$
$$4 \ v. \ 2$$
$$6 \ v. \ 3$$
$$5 \ v. \ 3$$
$$4 \ v. \ 3$$
$$3 \ v. \ 3$$

It is no longer absolutely necessary for the topics to be taught in the same order as they were originally but, again, passing will be the crucial topic on which success in the others will be built.

The only point that the teacher should insist on when further opponents are introduced is that neither an opponent nor a colleague should stand between server and receiver, so that the practice can get under way (Diag. 29). Also, in the early stages of these more difficult practices the teacher might ask the opponents to stand some distance away (about ten yards) from the receiver, but the skill level should be high enough to allow fairly close marking. Provided the first pass can be made without the ball being intercepted there should be no need for further restrictions.

The boys can be given some sort of target at this stage, apart from the number of consecutive passes made. It can be a goal, a skittle to knock down or merely a line to cross.

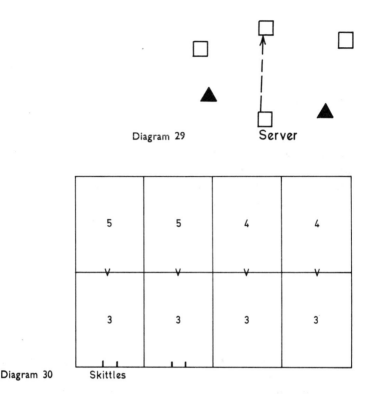

Diagram 29   Server

Diagram 30   Skittles

The group of five in the 5 *v*. 3 situations try to score a goal; when they do or when the opponents get the ball, the practice is repeated. Both groups in the 4 *v*. 3 situation try to get the ball across their opponents' line under control (Diagram 30).

The value of intelligent calling becomes increasingly evident when further opponents are introduced. The player in possession needs help from his colleagues, not only by their intelligent positioning, but also by their timely and relevant calls. They will also appreciate the importance of keeping quiet; of not asking for a pass because they are closely marked.

12 : Games

Games of various kinds should take up at least half of every lesson. They should be a natural extension of the SKILL section of the lessons, so that there is a possibility of 'transfer' of the techniques the boys have been practising into the games situation.

Five- or Six-a-side Game

The basic game will be the five- or six-a-side game played in a restricted area and with a minimum of rules so that continuous play is possible. Generally the teams should be of mixed ability, but there may be times when they are selected according to ability, so that the better players are put into situations where their superior skill has a chance to develop under more competitive conditions. Providing this does not become a regular practice, the less gifted players should not feel that they are being rejected.

From time to time a whole lesson might be devoted to a knock-out competition or a league table might be run over a period of weeks. The really cold, raw days that can occur during an English winter, when the practice of techniques becomes difficult, can be used for this purpose. Whenever competitions are held the teams should be evenly balanced. If the teacher finds that one team is carrying all before it, he can turn 'manager' and arrange some 'transfers'. On the other hand the SKILL section of the lesson should not be totally neglected during the colder months as continuity is vital if real progress is to be made.

RULES

These will vary according to where the game is played, but they will generally be kept to a minimum.

There should be no 'off-side' rule. Normal throw-ins can be taken or the ball can be side-footed or rolled along the ground into play.

A lot of time can be wasted with young players by insisting on the correct throw-in; they are interested in getting on with the game. Corners can be kicked or thrown in or even omitted altogether.

The important thing is the 'spirit of the game'.

There is no reason why small-side games should not be refereed by boys; in fact, it is suggested that this should be the common practice so that the teacher can concentrate on teaching. The boys should, of course, be trained to do this. There will always be days during an English winter when it isn't possible to play and this time can be utilised to teach the boys the basic rules.

If a complete set of rules is required for a competition of some kind, the following is suitable for use with younger players:

RULES FOR INTER-SOCCER TOURNAMENT

Five- or Six-a-side Football

Rules for a Competition

1 The ball is size 4 and the type agreed by both teams.

2 A team consists of five or six players, one of whom must be a goalkeeper.

One substitute is allowed if a player is unable to continue.

3 The equipment of a player consists of a shirt, vest or jersey, shorts, stockings and footwear appropriate to the playing surface.

4 The duration of the game is two equal periods, the length of each half to be decided between the teams.

5 The game commences by the ball being thrown out by a goal-

keeper. When a goal is scored the game recommences the same way.

6 When a ball is played over the side lines the game is restarted by a member of the opposing team rolling the ball into play underarm. A ball played over the goal line by an attacker or defender is returned to play by the goalkeeper rolling it with an underarm action.

7 There is no off-side.

8 Only the defending goalkeeper is allowed inside his goal area and he may handle the ball only in this area.

Penalty for Infringement:
  (a) by the defence, a penalty kick.
  (b) by the attack, a free kick at the point of entry into the circle.

All other infringements—indirect free kick.

Accidental entry by any player into a goal area which has no effect on the course of the game *is not* penalised.

9 A goal can be scored from anywhere outside the goal area.

10 No corners are awarded—but the referee keeps account of them. In the event of a draw, then the corners awarded are taken into account, and the team with the higher number shall be the winner. If both are equal the game shall continue until the first goal or corner (Sudden Death).

11 Charging is forbidden.

The game is controlled by a referee whose decisions on points of fact connected with the game shall be final, so far as the result of the game is concerned.

12 DIMENSIONS:
Playing area. Any size, but at a playing field it will normally be played across half a football pitch. In a playground netball markings are suitable.

Goals   The goals are 12 ft. long by 4 ft. high.

Goal area   The goal area is a semi-circle of 20 ft. radius.

CONDITIONED GAMES

In these games a 'condition' is imposed on the basic five- or six-a-side game so that the attention of the boys is focused on a particular aspect of the game. Only one conditioned game should be used in any one lesson and only for about five minutes.

The 'condition' imposed can be related to the particular skill being taught. Here are some examples:

PASSING

    i The ball mustn't go above waist height. This ensures that the ball is played with the feet.

    ii A player can only touch the ball twice before passing it. This condition prevents boys holding on to the ball too long.

    iii The ball must be passed with the inside of the foot

    iv The ball must be passed with the outside of the foot or the toe-end.

    v No pass should be more than five yards. This cuts out long, aimless passes.

CONTROL

    The ball must be controlled before it is passed. The game becomes totally unrealistic unless the boys are told to use the particular method of control appropriate to the situation.

BASIC TACTICS

    i A boy must never stand still after he has passed the ball.

    ii The passer of the ball must call 'HOLD' or 'PASS' to the receiver.

    iii The player in possession must try and 'take on' an opponent.

HEADING

    i A goal can only be scored with a header.

    ii All returns on to the field must be made with a header—including corners and goal kicks.

CHALLENGING

The player in possession must try and 'take on' an opponent. This condition, as used in the Basic Tactics section, will obviously encourage challenging.

OTHER GAMES

There are numerous games that include techniques from soccer or other games that can be played to increase the general level of skill and tactical awareness. Here are a few:

1. Football Tennis

This is played with teams of three or four using the markings described in Chapter 3 (Diags. 2, 3 and 4). Four games involving thirty-two players can be played in the area. The 'net' can be a piece of string about three to four feet high, between two netball posts. The rules can be made to suit the level of skill of the players.

In its simplest form the ball is allowed to bounce once before it is returned with any part of the body except the hands. It can, however, be modified to allow two or three contacts on one side with or without a bounce between each contact. The game is started with an underhand throw from the base line and can be played by any of the receiving team. If the teacher wants to encourage heading he can insist that the ball is returned with a header. The boys will have to use the other contacts to get the ball into a position for someone to return with a header.

2. Heading Tennis

This is played with a team of three or four using the same courts as the previous games but raising the 'net' to four to six feet. Only headers can be used. Again, the rules can be made to suit the ability of the player. The ball can be returned first time or it can be headed two or three times before being returned. A light plastic ball should be used.

3. Heading and Throwing

The rules are basically those for skittle ball, except that the player receiving the thrown ball heads it instead of catching it. It is thus collected by someone else who throws it for someone else to head. The sequence is, Throw—Head—Catch. A goal can only be scored by a header. The goal can be a circle on the wall, a hoop suspended from a netball post or even a normal six-a-side goal. The latter will encourage the boys to head downwards to score.

4. Extra Player Games

In these games an extra player joins whichever side has possession of the ball. Thus, in a five-a-side game, the team in possession has six players but loses him to the other side as soon as they are successfully challenged. With less skilful players there can be as many as three extra players.

This game helps to convince boys of the importance of good passing and control to retain possession of the ball.

5. Uneven Team Games

Sides of uneven size play each other but have different targets. For example in a 4 *v.* 2 game the four might be asked either:

(a) to attack a smaller goal or
(b) score in a more difficult way, e.g. control the ball over their opponents' goal line while their opponents score normally.

This game again stresses the importance of possession and the importance of an outnumbered team 'containing' or 'jockeying' its opponents.

Any games involving passing with the hands and running can be used to stress basic tactics. There are, of course, numerous such games suitable for young schoolboys many of which will be part of a sound and comprehensive games programme. Examples of such games are skittleball and basketball.

13 : Goalkeeping

All the goalkeeping practices in this chapter are easily related to the outfield practices in the relevant chapter.

Chapter Two. Opening Activities

In most of these practices a potential goalkeeper pairs up with an outfield player.

Practice 1. (Ball to each boy)
The goalkeeper rolls the ball along the ground and gathers it while moving among the other players.

Practice 2. (Ball to each boy)
As for the previous practice, but on gathering the ball the goalkeeper dodges to avoid interference from other players.

Practice 3. (Ball to each boy)
As for the previous practice, but the ball is rolled against a wall (if in a playground) and gathered on the rebound.

Practice 4. (Ball between two boys about five metres apart)
One boy passes the ball with his foot as they move among the other players; the other gathers the ball and returns it with an underarm roll.

71. Collecting a low rolling ball. The feet are in line with the ball, the legs straight and together, ball curled up to the chest (page 132).

72. Distributing a low rolling ball. The knees are bent and the foot opposite the throwing arm advanced towards the target: follow through in direction of the target (page 132).

Chapter Five — Passing and Distributing a Low Rolling Ball

(a) Practice of Techniques without Opposition

Practice 1. (Ball between two boys about five metres apart)
The goalkeeper rolls the ball along the ground to his partner who controls it before returning it with a pass with the inside of the foot (Photos 71 and 72). The goalkeeper collects it from a standing position.

Common Faults in Collecting the Ball

i The goalkeeper does not get his feet directly in line with the approaching ball.

His legs must form a further barrier should the ball elude his hands and arms.

ii The feet are directly in line with the approaching ball but the legs are 'bowed' sideways as the ball is gathered. The second line of defence is thus of little use.

The legs must always remain in line with the approaching ball.

iii The arms and hands are held too far apart.

The elbows must be pulled inwards and the hands held close together with the palms, fingers spread, turned and towards the ball. The 'channel' formed by the hands and arms allows the ball to be curled up to the chest.

iv The ball is not 'hugged' to the chest.

The forearms, with elbows together, should prevent the ball leaving the chest, and the outspread fingers on top of the ball will prevent it moving upwards.

Common Faults to look for in Distributing the Ball

i The foot opposite the throwing arm is not advanced towards the target.

ii The goalkeeper faces his target squarely.

He should half turn towards it as he advances his foot. This allows a more controlled and powerful pass.

iii The knees are not bent.

If the rear knee is bent so that it almost touches the ground, the ball can be released close to the ground and will not bounce.

iv The throwing arm is moved across the body.

It should move straight towards the target both in the delivery and the follow-through.

Practice 2. (Ball between two boys about five metres apart)
The goalkeeper rolls the ball along the ground to his partner who returns it with a first time pass with the inside of the foot. The ball is collected from a kneeling position (Photo 73).

73. Collecting from the kneeling position. The body is behind the ball, one foot turned sideways towards the ball and no gap between that foot and the other knee.

Common Faults—Corrections

i The goalkeeper does not get his body behind the ball. This method of collection is more often used when the ball is approaching quickly and when the goalkeeper has to move some distance to collect it. He must, therefore, move quickly into position.

ii The left foot (for a ball travelling to the left of the goalkeeper) is not placed directly in the line of the approaching ball and with the inside of the foot facing it.

iii The right knee is not placed on the ground just behind the left foot. There will then be a gap through which the ball can pass.

iv The arms and hands are held too far apart as in the previous practice.

v The ball is not 'hugged' to the chest as in the previous practice.

vi The goalkeeper does not stand up as soon as he has collected the ball safely.

He must be in the standing position in order to distribute the ball quickly.

Practice 3. (Ball between two boys about five metres apart)
As for the previous practices, except that the goalkeeper decides which of the two types of collection to use. He distributes it in the same way each time.

Common Faults—Corrections

Apart from faults already described, the main one will now be slowness in deciding which type of collection to use.

The goalkeeper must quickly assess the type of ball he is receiving, and use the appropriate collection technique. Even in this simple situation he has a decision to make!

Practice 4. (Ball between two boys about five metres apart)
The boys move anywhere in the playing area, and the goalkeeper

collects the ball from his partner's passes, using either technique, before returning it along the ground.

Common Faults—Corrections

i The goalkeeper concentrates too much on his partner. He must get into the habit of observing what is going on around them.

ii He always allows the ball to come to him.

Whenever possible, he should move towards it to collect it and so prevent an interception.

iii He stands still after collecting the ball.

He should move his body away from any 'trouble' and move quickly into a space from where he can distribute the ball.

iv The ball is distributed carelessly.

Like any outfield player he must distribute the ball so that his partner can control it easily. Careless distribution by a goal-keeper can be much more serious than by an outfield player.

(b) Small Group Practices with Opposition

The goalkeeper joins in these practices for passing techniques along with the other members of the class but, instead of collecting and distributing the ball with his feet, he uses the techniques just described. When he is the opponent he tries to touch the ball with hands or feet or even collect it. The faults of the practices without opposition will occur more readily when an opponent is introduced and must be corrected. In addition:

i The ball is distributed regardless of the position of the opponent.

The goalkeeper, like the outfield player, should distribute the ball away from the opponent's line of approach.

ii The goalkeeper is not aware of the proximity of the opponent when he receives the ball.

He must be encouraged to look around so that he can decide when to distribute the ball. He will either distribute it quickly or dodge into a space before distributing it.

Chapter Six – Control

Collecting and Distributing a Low Bouncing Ball

(a) Practice of Techniques without Opposition

Practice 1. (Ball between two boys, five to ten metres apart)
The goalkeeper throws the ball to his partner with a one-handed
throw from the shoulder (Photo 74). His partner controls it and
returns it with a two-handed underarm throw that bounces below
knee height.

74. Distributing a ball from the shoulder. The knees are bent
and the foot opposite the throwing arm advanced: follow
through in direction of the target.

Faults to look for in Collecting the Ball
As for collecting a low rolling ball.

Faults to look for in Distributing the Ball

i The steadying or non-throwing hand is taken away too quickly.

Although this is described as a one-handed throw, the other hand must steady the ball at the front and only be taken away as the thrust forward from the shoulder is made.

ii The foot opposite the throwing arm is not advanced towards the target.

iii The knees are not bent.

This must be done so that the ball is distributed from as near the ground as possible.

iv The throwing arm is moved across the body.

v The goalkeeper faces his target squarely.

Practice 2. (Ball between two boys, eight to ten metres apart)
As for the previous practice except that the ball is either bounced to the goalkeeper, as in the previous practice, or rolled along the ground.

Common Faults—Corrections
As for the previous practice.

Practice 3. (Ball between two boys about eight to ten metres apart)
The boys move anywhere in the playing area and the goalkeeper's partner serves either balls along the ground or low bouncing balls. The goalkeeper uses what he thinks is the appropriate method of collection and distribution.

Common Faults—Corrections
These have been described in the previous practices.

(b) Small Group Practices with Opposition

The goalkeeper joins in these practices for control techniques but instead of collecting and distributing with his feet he uses the techniques just described. As the opponent he again tries to touch the ball with his hands or feet or even collect it. The faults of the practices without opposition will occur more readily.

Collecting and Distributing a Ball at Lower Chest or Abdomen Height

Practice 1. (Ball between two boys about five metres apart)
The ball is served to the goalkeeper with a two-handed basketball bounce pass so that it rises fairly steeply. He collects it and returns it to his partner in the same way (Photos 75 and 76).

Common Faults—Corrections

i The hands are not offered to the approaching ball.

They should be held out, palms upwards and forearms quite close together, so that the ball cannot fall between them.

ii The ball is not 'hugged' to the abdomen or lower chest.

As soon as the ball passes from the outstretched hands, the arms are curled towards the body.

iii The goalkeeper remains in an upright position.

His upper body should be arched over the ball so that it cannot move upwards.

Practice 2. (Ball between two boys about 5–6 metres apart)
The goalkeeper receives different types of services so that he has to collect the ball in any of *three* ways already practised.

Common Faults—Corrections

All the faults have been described for the different types of collection.

Practice 3. (Ball between two boys about 5–6 metres apart)
The boys move anywhere in the playing area and the goalkeeper's partner varies the serve so that any of the three methods of collection are used. The goalkeeper distributes the ball in either of the two ways he has practised or with a basketball bounce pass to give his partner practice of control with the chest or abdomen.

Common Faults—Corrections: Already described.

75. The hands are offered to the approaching ball with forearms close together.

76. The ball is hugged to the chest and the body arched over it.

(b) Small Group Practices with Opposition

The goalkeeper joins in the practice along with other members of the class, but collects and distributes the ball with his hands. As the opponent he tries to intercept the ball with hands or feet.

Common Faults—Corrections
The faults of the practices without opposition will occur more readily when an opponent is introduced. The goalkeeper, as in the passing topic, should look around so that he knows where the opponent is and where to distribute the ball. He must also decide which type of collection and distribution to use.

Collecting and Distributing a High Dropping Ball

(a) Practice of Techniques without Opposition

Practice 1. (Ball between two boys 5–6 metres apart)
The ball is lobbed to the goalkeeper with a two-handed underarm throw so that it drops towards his chest. He collects it and returns it in the same way.

Common Faults—Corrections

i The goalkeeper does not get underneath the dropping ball.
He should be underneath the ball, feet about 18 inches apart and slightly bent.

ii He does not offer his hands to the dropping ball.
They should be held upwards and slightly forwards with fingers spread. The forearm and hands are close together.

iii The ball is not 'hugged' to the chest.
As soon as the ball reaches the hands the fingers spread round it and the arms are curled towards the body.

iv The goalkeeper remains in the upright position.
As soon as the ball is safely hugged to his chest he bends his knee and arches his body over the ball so that it cannot be dislodged.

Practice 2. (Ball between two boys 5–6 yards apart)
The goalkeeper receives different types of service so that he has to collect the ball in any of the *four* ways already practised.

Common Faults—Corrections
Already discussed.

Practice 3. (Ball between two boys 5–6 metres apart)
As for the previous practice except that the boys move anywhere in the playing area.

Common Faults—Corrections
Already discussed.

(b) Small Group Practices with Opposition

Chapter Seven – Basic Tactics

All of the teaching of this topic is done through small group practices with opposition, in groups of 3 *v*. 1. The work should be done on grass and all boys should be in soft shoes, e.g. plimsolls.

Movement off the Ball

When the goalkeeper is not an opponent he can practice the four methods of collection and the two methods of distribution.

When he is the opponent there will be plenty of opportunities to practice:

> (a) the 'basic ready' position,
> (b) diving.

(a) *The 'Basic ready' position*
This is a position of alertness which allows the goalkeeper to move most efficiently into the twists, turns, dives and jumps necessary to make saves in the games situation (Photo 77).

77. Basic Ready position.

78. Hands behind the ball passing overhead (p. 144).

He stands with his feet about shoulder-width apart, trunk leaning forward slightly and his arms held forward.

Common Faults—Corrections

i The goalkeeper is too upright.

He should be in a crouched position which will allow him to deal more efficiently with a ball close to the body. This is also a better position from which to make a dive to either side.

ii He holds his hands by his sides.

They should be held up, bent at the elbows, so that the forearms are roughly parallel to the ground and the hands half-turned to the field of play.

(b) *Diving to one side*

In the 3 *v.* 1 situation the goalkeeper, as the one opponent, treats every pass as a shot at goal and tries to collect, deflect or touch them. As the boys will be working in a limited area, the goalkeeper will be kept very busy and must react quickly. From the 'basic ready' position he dives sideways and tries to get both hands behind the ball. In practice he will usually manage to get the lower hand to the ball first but the other hand should quickly follow to produce a more effective barrier.

Common Faults—Corrections

i The goalkeeper dives on to his stomach instead of his side.

By diving on his side his body is a more effective barrier, he can reach further and he is less likely to hurt himself.

Movement with the Ball

This 3 *v.* 1 situation, in which the three are encouraged to take the ball to the opponent, inviting him to make a tackle, lends itself to the goalkeeper practising *diving at the feet*. As the opponent he tries to prevent the boy with the ball dribbling past him or making a pass, by diving at his feet.

Common Faults—Corrections

i The goalkeeper commits himself to a dive at the wrong time.

From the 'basic ready' position he moves towards the player with the ball. If this player loses control of the ball, however slightly, he may be able to move in quickly and dive for the ball. If the player doesn't lose control of the ball he should approach more slowly, attempting to guide the player to one side.

He makes his dive to the one side when the player is about two yards away.

ii He dives in such a way that only his arms are a barrier to the ball.

When the player with the ball is about two yards away and being guided to one side the goalkeeper sinks on his side in that direction so that the ball is covered by his lower chest and abdomen.

iii He remains in the position in which he has received the ball.

As soon as the ball comes to rest against his lower chest and abdomen he should curl up so that his legs and arms close around it. He then rolls over so that his back faces the player who had the ball.

Chapter Eight – Heading

Collecting the Ball Passing Overhead

(a) Practice of Techniques without Opposition

Practice 1. (Ball between two boys about 4–5 metres apart)
The ball is served to the goalkeeper with an underhand throw so that he can collect it above his head without jumping (Photo 78). He returns it so that the outfield player can head it forward from a standing position. After ten services to the goalkeeper he now serves ten balls so that his partner can head them back.

Common Faults—Corrections

i The arms are not raised with the hands together.

The thumbs should be touching and the fingers spread out behind the ball.

ii The ball is not brought down to the chest quickly.

As the ball touches the outspread hands the fingers spread round it and the wrists and the elbows are bent so that the ball is brought down, and hugged to the chest.

iii The forearms are held too wide apart.

As the hands move round the ball as it is hugged to the chest,

79. Jumping for a ball and catching it in front of the head (page 146).

the forearms are brought close together so that the ball cannot slip down between them.

iv The eyes are not kept on the ball.

This, of course, is vital.

Practice 2. (Ball between two boys, 4–5 metres apart)
As for the previous practice, except that the ball is served to the goalkeeper so that he must jump for it (Photo 79).

Common Faults—Corrections
As for the previous practice. In addition:

i The jump is mistimed.

The goalkeeper should try to time his jump so that he catches the ball as high as possible.

ii The goalkeeper catches the ball immediately above his head.

He should catch it above and just in front of his head so that he can see it.

Practice 3. (Ball between two boys about 4–5 metres apart)
The goalkeeper is now served several balls he can either collect with a jump or from a standing position. The ball can be served from a frontal or side position. The latter will enable the goalkeeper to get practice in dealing with balls crossing the goal.

Common Faults—Corrections

i As for the previous practice, but now the goalkeeper has a decision to make as to whether to jump or not.

ii The goalkeeper completely faces the direction from which the ball is being crossed.

He should only be half-turned to the ball. This will enable him to deal with the longer ball for which he has to move sideways across the goal until he is in the position to jump and turn in the same movement to catch the ball (Photos 80 and 81).

80. The goalkeeper is half-turned towards the ball.

81. He jumps to collect the ball on full stretch.

(b) Small Group Practices with Opposition

The goalkeeper joins in these practices for heading techniques along with other members of the class. As an opponent he first attempts to intercept the header and then the passes with the feet.

As one of the group he first collects the high ball served to him and then collects and distributes the ball using the appropriate technique.

Common Faults—Corrections

The faults of the technique without opposition will occur more frequently.

As there is an opponent the goalkeeper is more likely to take his eye off the ball.

It is also vital that he catches the ball at full height so that the opponent does not first reach it with his head.

In the early stage it may be necessary to place the server and opponent more than five to six yards away in order to give the goalkeeper more time to make his save.

Chapter Nine — Challenging

All of the teaching in this topic is done through the small group practice with opposition in the narrow lanes or 'corridors'. The work is done on grass, and all boys should wear soft shoes, e.g. plimsolls.

As the opponent, the goalkeeper tries to win the ball from the two attackers by any means. The attackers in their turn try to beat him by any means—passing, dribbling or shooting.

Common Faults—Corrections

The goalkeeper will be called upon to use the various techniques he has practised, but in a highly competitive situation many of the faults already described will occur more readily.

In addition:

i He commits himself to a challenge too readily.

He should try and sum up the situation and make his challenge when the attackers lose close control of the ball, when there is a shot, or when a player tries to dribble past him.

Appendix 1   Useful Addresses

The Football Association, 16 Lancaster Gate, London, W2 3LW. *Telephone:* 01 262 4542.

The F.A. runs courses for coaches and teachers and holiday coaching courses for boys aged 14–16. Write for details. The F.A. also runs a proficiency award scheme for schoolchildren, which is called the Super Skills Awards Scheme. Write for details.

English Schools' Football Association, 4A Eastgate Street, Stafford, Staffs. *Telephone:* Stafford 51142.

The E.S.F.A. is the Governing Body for schools football in England and runs its own proficiency award scheme as well as supporting fully the F.A.'s scheme. Write for details.

Women's Football Association, 7 Mayfield Road, Hornsey, London, N8. *Telephone:* 01 340 6661.

There are still not many girls who get the opportunity to play football at school but it is on the increase and the W.F.A. is responsible for an increasing amount of organised competitive football.

The Football Association of Wales, 3 Fairy Road, Wrexham, Clwyd. *Telephone:* Wrexham 2424.

Irish Football Association, 20 Windsor Avenue, Belfast. *Telephone:* Belfast 669458.

Scottish Football Association, 8 Gertrude Place, Barrhead, Glasgow. *Telephone:* Glasgow 4025.

Appendix 2

The English Schools' Football Association, which is the governing body for schools football in England has issued the following document which is considered to be a 'landmark in the work of the E.S.F.A.' In it they follow the format of a games lesson laid down in this book and recommend the book to teachers as a source for much of their lesson material.

With the advisory document the E.S.F.A. also issued a Code of Conduct for Schoolboys which if followed, would do much to counteract the kind of behaviour which sometimes characterises the game, even in schools but which is deplored by most teachers.

Advisory Document for Schools' Football for Boys 9–13 Years of Age

FOREWORD

While it is generally agreed that the foundation of Association Football is laid in the schools the Council of the E.S.F.A. is strong in its belief that it is in the teaching of 9–13 year old boys that our hopes for the future development of the game rest.

It is in these years that a boy's initial love for football should be engendered his early skills encouraged, and the fundamentals of good sportsmanship inculcated.

As in other aspects of education, it is the teacher who is responsible for the principles of the game being correctly absorbed, not only by the stars of tomorrow, but indeed by all the boys in his charge.

It is the duty of the teacher to encourage his boys to develop to the limit of their varying capabilities and it is to help him in this task that this advice is offered.

ATTITUDE TO THE GAME

It is stressed that one of the most important aims in football is to ensure that the true meaning and appreciation of good sportsmanship is understood and assimilated so completely that 'playing the game' becomes an integral part of the boy's character.

The all-embracing skills, disciplines, the willing acceptance of a referee's ruling, and the spirit of co-operation in a team situation—all these lead to the making of the all round sportsman who can gain enjoyment from the game regardless of his prowess.

At all times it is essential that the boy should be made aware that his first loyalty is to his school.

THE TEACHING SITUATION

Generally speaking the format of a games' lesson should consist of THREE parts:

- (a) Introductory Activity or 'Warm-up'.
- (b) Technique and skill teaching and practice—individually and in groups.
- (c) Small-sided games.

Considerable material is available for the content of lessons, particularly in *Teaching Soccer*.

It is important that the techniques and skills practised and developed in parts (a) and (b) should be placed into the actual game situation at an early stage. Indeed, it is to be hoped that the practices selected for part (b) will also be designed to involve realistic game situations.

The 'Games' section should be of a small-sided nature with 3-, 4-, 5-, 6- or 7-a-side teams enjoying a variety of conditioned games. It is perhaps wiser to reserve the 11-a-side game for the extra-curricular sessions.

THE COACHING SITUATION

The development of keener and probably more able boys will be better served by extra-curricular coaching sessions. (The attention to the particular needs of the school 'team' during lesson time is to be discouraged.) Using the teaching format and applying more flexibility the technique and skills of the boys can be developed to higher levels.

The publication *Tactics and Teamwork* will broaden the know-

ledge of the teacher and enable him to coach with mor
standing without reporting to 'systems of play' which can
somewhat stereotyped play.

COACHING COURSES

Adults

The development of both lessons and coaching sessions will
always be limited both by the teacher's knowledge and ability,
and the standard of the boys under control. While the ability of
the class can be restrictive, the teacher may take advantage of
Coaching Courses. It is recommended that P.E. Organisers and
F.A. Regional Coaches be approached to organise courses for
teachers (men and women) leading to the F.A. Teaching Certi-
ficate. Courses of this type usually prove very popular and their
value is invariably reflected in the confidence and standard of
instruction of the teacher, and in the subsequent enthusiasm and
raising of the standard of play among the pupils.

Boys

Apart from 'class' coaching sessions the organising of Coaching
Courses for selected and unselected boys of this age by Local
and/or County Associations is highly recommended. It is suggested that the co-operation, advice and assistance of P.E.
Organisers and F.A. Regional Coaches should also be sought.

INTER-SCHOOL AND INTER-ASSOCIATION GAMES

1 *Competitive Football*

While Council would recognise competitive football for the age
groups aimed at in this document, it would, at the same time,
point out the need for care to be taken in arranging fixtures so
that there is no excessive travelling. Further, Council would stress
that teachers should always shield the young footballer from un-

due strain of any kind—both physical and mental. Efforts should be made to ensure that the schoolboy is never engaged in the playing of two matches on the same day. Council would even question the advisability of a young player taking part in competitive games on consecutive days.

It is acknowledged that boys will receive instruction in tactical play, but it is hoped that this instruction will be kept to a minimum. In other words, a loose pattern should be presented to the boy, within which framework he may develop his skills and individual style. Too often team coaches inadvertently regiment their teams to such an extent that play becomes stereotyped so that the joy and thrill of experiment becomes lost.

Attention is called to the following extract from Football Association Rule 29 (Schoolboys and Associated Schoolboys):

(iii) Boys who are under 9 years of age on 1st September in any playing season shall not be allowed to participate in competitions sanctioned by The Football Association or its constituent County Football Associations.

(iv) A player who is over 9 years and under 14 years on 1st September in any playing season should not play in a team involving players who are more than two years older than himself.

Football for players in this age grouping should be arranged within the following age bands:

1. Over 9 years, Under 11 years
2. Over 10 years, Under 12 years
3. Over 11 years, Under 13 years
4. Over 12 years, Under 14 years

2. *Kit*

It is urged that every effort be made by the teacher to ensure that his boys are properly and smartly kitted out, and that advice is given regarding the advisability of the wearing of shin guards, and the correct fitting and lacing of boots, etc. Future good habits depend on these important points.

3. *Size of Ball*

A size 3 (or a *new* size 4) ball should be used for all games.

4. *Ground Measurements*

Council strongly recommends that, wherever possible, the following measurements be used for 11-a-side games:

Size of Pitch	70–80 metres long (75–85 yards)
	40–50 metres wide (45–55 yards)
Size of Goals	6½ metres wide (7 yards)
	2 metres high (6 ft. 6 in.)

Penalty Area—to be reduced to two-thirds of normal size.
Penalty spot to be 9 metres (10 yards) from the goal line.
The playing of matches should not take place on full size pitches.

5. *Duration of Play*

The duration of play in any schools' match, including extra time if necessary, shall not exceed 30 minutes each way.

6. *Referees*

It is to be hoped that, as for more senior games, Referees will make every effort to be suitably attired, and should control the game strictly according to the Laws. However it is strongly urged that Referees should make sure that the boys fully understand the reasons, should an infringement occur.
It is imperative that the players should respect the Referee, accept his ruling unquestioningly and play the game according to the Laws.

Once again, the responsibility for ensuring that these virtues are so absorbed by the boy as to become habits, rests upon the Teacher. Not only must he inculcate the correct attitude into the boy, but he should be always on his guard to protect the young footballer from undesirable influences with which he may come into contact in *any* of his footballing activities.

RECOMMENDED PUBLICATIONS AND FILMS

There are a number of publications and films available which should prove of value in the teaching and coaching of boys. Details can be found in the E.S.F.A. Handbook or an information sheet can be obtained from the General Secretary on receipt of a stamped addressed envelope.

The two publications mentioned in this document can be obtained as follows:

(i) *Teaching Soccer* by Alan Gibbon and John Cartwright, Bell and Hyman Ltd.

(ii) *Tactics and Teamwork* from The Football Association, 16 Lancaster Gate, London, W2 3LW.

CONCLUSION

The Council of the English Schools' F.A. will at all times welcome pertinent observations and questions from the Membership relating to all aspects of the game, and in particular, observations on the age area aimed at in this Document.

Code of Conduct for Schoolboys

1 Learn and observe the Laws of the Game.

2 Beat opponents by skill and not by unfair methods.

3 Never argue with the Referee or Linesmen.

4 Retire quickly to 10 yards when a free kick is given against you.

5 Do not appeal for throw-ins, off-sides, free-kicks, etc.

6 Give the ball promptly to opponents for throw-ins, free-kicks, etc.

7 If an opponent gives you the ball for a throw-in, free-kick, etc., do not take advantage of him being out of position.

8 Keep your self-control at all times and do not retaliate.

9 Do not overact when your team scores a goal.

10 Accept victory modestly and defeat cheerfully.